THE BATTLE
OF
FISHER'S HILL

THE BATTLE
OF
FISHER'S HILL

Breaking the Shenandoah Valley's Gibraltar

JONATHAN A. NOYALAS

Charleston ┤ ├ London

THE
History
PRESS

Published by The History Press
Charleston, SC 29403
www.historypress.net

Front cover: Sheridan's cavalry at the Battle of Fisher's Hill (Shenandoah Valley), published by Currier & Ives, circa 1864. *Courtesy of the American Antiquarian Society.*

First published 2013

Manufactured in the United States

ISBN 978.1.60949.443.8

Library of Congress CIP data applied for.

This book is dedicated to the cadre of history professors who years ago mentored me and showed unceasing support for my endeavors, especially Brandon H. Beck, William C. "Jack" Davis, Warren Hofstra, James I. "Bud" Robertson Jr. and Catherine Tisinger.

Contents

Preface

In 1957, the year that the United States Congress authorized the establishment of the Civil War Centennial Commission, southern writer Walker Percy observed that trying to understand the Civil War and its meaning "is like a man walking away from a mountain. The bigger it is, the farther he's got to go before he can see it. Then one day he looks back and there it is, this colossal thing lying across his past."[1] Since the conflict's end, Americans have been trying to understand that great "colossal" moment of our national epic and come to terms with its results. The quest for answers about our nation's bloodiest struggle has produced thousands of volumes over the decades that have addressed a wide array of topics examining the Civil War from various perspectives, such as military, political, social and gender history. Remarkably, in the thousands of books written about the conflict, there are still deficiencies in the historiography, in which pivotal moments have not been addressed with great attention. This book attempts to address one of those paucities and bring to light, for the first time in a singular study, a history of the Battle of Fisher's Hill.

The earliest chroniclers of the Battle of Fisher's Hill were Union veterans who fought with the Army of the Shenandoah in the autumn of 1864. While those veterans had a vested interest in telling the battle's story for the sake of their own legacy, some seemed shocked that the second battle of General Philip H. Sheridan's 1864 Shenandoah Campaign received scant attention from historians. Veteran Aldace Walker, an officer in the stalwart Vermont Brigade, noted very simply that "this battle has faded almost entirely from the memory of the average reader…and has been almost entirely overlooked by our historians."[2]

In the decades after the conflict, only a few authors—most notably George E. Pond, the associate editor of the *Army and Navy Journal*, and prolific author and wartime correspondent Charles Carleton Coffin—paid any significant attention to the Battle of Fisher's Hill. Pond discussed the tactical ebb and flow of the battle in *The Shenandoah Valley in 1864*, published in 1883. Seven years later, Coffin addressed the battle in his *Freedom Triumphant: The Fourth Period of the War of the Rebellion*. Not until 1987, with the release of Jeffry D. Wert's seminal study *From Winchester to Cedar Creek*, however, did the battle receive its first significant attention—although as a component of a much larger work. Since the publication of Wert's larger campaign study, only a handful of historians, such as Scott Patchan, Robert E.L. Krick and I, have written and published about the battle, albeit in article or essay format.

Nearly a decade ago, on a visit to the Ramseur's Hill parcel at Fisher's Hill with my great friend Richard Sturtz, the idea coursed through my mind to write a book about this battle and its consequences. Other academic endeavors intervened, however, and distracted me from the project. As the Civil War sesquicentennial neared, Terry Heder, another good friend and a tireless advocate for battlefield preservation with the Shenandoah Valley Battlefields Foundation, inquired if I had any intention of writing a book on Fisher's Hill and, if so, whether I could get it done in time for the battle's anniversary. Already having an active role in the foundation as chair of the committee on interpretation and education in the interpretive planning of that battlefield, I realized the time had come.

In constructing this first-ever volume on the Battle of Fisher's Hill and as part of The History Press's Sesquicentennial Series, I wanted to produce a book—working within the series' framework—that not only told the story of the battle and discussed troop movements but also examined the attitudes of both Union and Confederate soldiers leading up to, during and after the fight. Furthermore, I wanted to illustrate how the civilians in the battle's path—especially those living in Strasburg and the hamlet of Fisher's Hill—reacted to and were impacted by the fight. Additionally, I desired to show how this battle greatly boosted spirits in the North while simultaneously examine the range of reactions to the defeat among Confederates. Lastly, I wanted to produce a book that looked beyond the battle and its immediate consequences to show how the battlefield's landscape in the decades after the war emerged as a spot for postwar reunions of Union and Confederate veterans and served as a stage for reconciliation among former foes.

The events surrounding the battle and its legacy are constructed from predominantly primary source material, both published and in archival collections, including regimental histories, battle reports, newspaper accounts, diaries, journals and letters—some of which are in private collections and being utilized here for the first time. Postwar reunion speeches and veterans' reminiscences helped in reconstructing the battlefield's postwar life as a gathering point for veterans of blue and gray.

Writing this book over the previous three years has been a tremendous undertaking and would not have been possible without the help of countless individuals. The people I recognize here have in some way contributed to this project but are in no way at fault for any of its errors: Nan Card at the Rutherford B. Hayes Presidential Center in Fremont, Ohio, who has always been supportive of my research endeavors; Linden "Butch" Fravel, who eagerly shared things with me related to the Steele family; David Garms, who shared his own research about the Funkhouser family; Fred Molineux, a descendant of Colonel Molineux, who always willingly shared letters and information about his ancestor; my dear friend and fine historian in his own right Nicholas Picerno (even if he does believe the Twenty-ninth Maine singlehandedly won the Civil War for the Union) for opening up his impressive collection for my use and who has been a constant and unflinching supporter of my work and research; friend and fellow board member of the Kernstown Battlefield Association Scott Patchan, who has my same passion for all things related to the Shenandoah Valley, for sharing newspaper articles from his files with me; Dr. Joseph Whitehorne, my friend and former colleague at Lord Fairfax Community College, for graciously sharing his advice and research on various historic resource studies done at Fisher's Hill; and Karen Wisecarver, the interlibrary loan specialist at my institution, Lord Fairfax Community College, who always goes above and beyond the call of duty. Last, but certainly not least, I would like to thank the two most important people in my life, whom I love more than words could ever express: my awesome son, Alexander, and my soul mate, best friend and love of my life, Brandy, a fine historian and teacher, whose research assistance and advice have been invaluable.

Introduction

Four years after the Civil War's end, Vermont veteran Aldace Walker published his *The Vermont Brigade in the Shenandoah Valley, 1864*. While Walker surmised that the Union victories at the Third Battle of Winchester and Cedar Creek would always remain "the best known of Sheridan's Valley battles" in the minds of most Americans and define the general's legacy in the nation's popular historical consciousness, he believed that some, if not all, of the Army of the Shenandoah's veterans might disagree. The Vermonter contended that most veterans favored Sheridan's triumph at the Battle of Fisher's Hill on September 22, 1864, as the seminal moment in Sheridan's and perhaps the Army of the Shenandoah's time in the Shenandoah Valley. Walker believed that "among his soldiers the idea was current, and still prevails, that the battle of Fisher's Hill, with its unusual amount of careful reconnoitering and skillful maneuvering, resulting in almost incredible success, displayed even more military genius than either of the first named fields."[3]

Among all of the battles fought as part of Sheridan's 1864 Shenandoah Campaign, the fight at Fisher's Hill proved to be a pivotal moment in the valley's wartime annals, as not only the most decisive Union victory achieved with such small human cost but also the Union triumph that opened the door for Sheridan to enact his campaign of devastation known as "the Burning." Aside from the battle's strategic gains, it boosted Republican morale enough for President Abraham Lincoln to win reelection in 1864 and defeat Democratic challenger George B. McClellan. In addition to the battle's military and political ramifications, it brought to the forefront the discontent that some Confederate soldiers and civilians in the Shenandoah Valley held for General Jubal A. Early and the Confederate command structure. That contempt grew to such a fevered pitch with the Confederate debacle at Fisher's Hill that a number of soldiers and civilians urged Confederate officials to remove Early from command in the vitally strategic region.

Beyond the engagement's wartime consequences, the Fisher's Hill battlefield emerged as a picturesque spot in the era of postwar reconciliation for veterans of Sheridan's and Early's armies to gather. On that once-contested battlefield, former foes came to engage in activities of remembrance to honor the men who sacrificed everything on that field. Former enemies also congregated there to partake in genuine acts of respect that helped heal the bitter wounds of war, thus transforming what once had been known as the "Gibraltar of the Valley" into perhaps a Gibraltar of national healing.

The story of the Battle of Fisher's Hill and the ground on which it was fought is significant not only to Shenandoah Valley regional history and Civil War history but also to the saga of the American historical epic. The battle, the landscape, the men of both Union and Confederate armies who fought and died there and later the veterans who returned to honor the fallen and be part of legitimate reconciliation activities serve as a great representation of the immense sacrifice of war while simultaneously and inspiringly offering hope for forgiveness and healing among bitter rivals.

Chapter One

"Lifting Itself Up Menacingly to Our Advance"

Throughout the first three years of the Civil War, Union military operations in Virginia's Shenandoah Valley, with a few exceptions, usually resulted in disaster. "To many a Federal general it had been the valley of humiliation," noted the Eighth Vermont's George Carpenter after the conflict, "on account of the defeats his forces had suffered. Neither Patterson, Banks, Shields, Fremont, Milroy, Sigel nor Crook had been able to destroy the enemy west of the Blue Ridge."[4]

Until the late summer of 1864, the Shenandoah Valley supported the Confedcrate war effort in a variety of ways. First, the region's crop outputs supplied significant amounts of foodstuffs to Confederate armies in Virginia. In addition to its role as the "Breadbasket of the Confederacy," the valley also served as an avenue of invasion for Confederate armies into the North and a point from which those same armies could threaten Washington, D.C. Consequently, at various points in the war, Confederate war planners in Richmond looked to the Shenandoah Valley as a place to create a strategic diversion and alleviate pressure against Richmond. General Thomas J. "Stonewall" Jackson used the valley as a diversionary theater in the spring of 1862, and General Jubal Early attempted to do the same in the summer of 1864.[5]

By late July 1864, Union general in chief Ulysses S. Grant fumed over the inability of Union forces in the Shenandoah Valley to secure the region, prevent its provender from feeding Confederate armies and preclude its use as a diversionary theater of war. Grant understood that until he could silence

Early's Confederate forces in the valley, he would not be able to strike the necessary death blow to General Robert E. Lee's Army of Northern Virginia in front of Petersburg and thus open the gates to Richmond. Following Early's victory at the Second Battle of Kernstown on July 24, 1864, and General John McCausland's burning of Chambersburg, Pennsylvania, six days later, Grant determined to create a massive force under a competent general to crush Early's army.[6]

After Grant determined to silence Confederate forces in the valley, he reflected on why the Shenandoah had been the scene of so many Union disasters. Grant believed they had occurred due to several factors. First, Grant observed that officials in Washington, D.C., did not fully understand the Shenandoah Valley's strategic significance. To Grant, it seemed as if the War Department viewed the valley solely as a buffer for the capital. "It seemed to be the policy of General Halleck and Secretary Stanton, to keep any force sent there, in pursuit of the invading army," Grant noted, "moving right and left so as to keep between the enemy and our capital; and, generally speaking they pursued this policy until all knowledge of the whereabouts of the enemy was lost."[7] Additionally, Grant understood that at no point in the conflict did the various Union armies either in the Shenandoah Valley or the immediate surrounding region make any efforts to cooperate with one another. Incensed over these issues, Grant aimed to do something about it.

In an attempt to create a cohesive army with numerical superiority to Early's command, Grant consolidated four departments—Department of the Susquehanna, Middle Department, Department of Washington and Department of the West—into the Middle Military Division. Now with an army of around forty thousand, Grant next needed a competent and aggressive general to command it.

When Grant met with President Abraham Lincoln and Secretary of War Edwin M. Stanton to discuss potential candidates to command this new Middle Military Division, he initially suggested Major General William B. Franklin, a fellow classmate of Grant's at West Point. Lincoln disapproved of this choice. A Democrat, Franklin constantly criticized the Lincoln administration and had his reputation tarnished by the debacle of his Left Grand Division at the Battle of Fredericksburg in December 1862. Additionally, Lincoln did not like the choice because Franklin supported former Union general George B. McClellan for president.[8] Lincoln understood that the result of the campaign in the Shenandoah Valley would contribute to his success or failure at the polls in November. After Franklin, Grant suggested Major General George G. Meade, the current commander of the Army of the Potomac. Lincoln also disliked this idea. The president reminded Grant that a number of individuals had pressured him to remove Meade from command. With the election only months away, Lincoln did not want to appear as if he caved into the wishes of a few individuals.[9] Finally, Grant suggested Major General Philip H. Sheridan. Lincoln appeared comfortable with the decision, but Stanton

General Philip H. Sheridan, commander of the Army of the Shenandoah. *Author's collection.*

did not. Although Sheridan was a West Point graduate and had performed well with Grant in the West and as a cavalry commander in the Army of the Potomac, Stanton believed that Sheridan was too young for such an important post, particularly months away from Lincoln's reelection bid. Grant, however, calmed Stanton's fears, and Sheridan became the commander of the newly minted Middle Military Division, popularly referred to as the Army of the Shenandoah, on August 6, 1864.

After nearly one month of organizing and maneuvering with Early's army between Harper's Ferry and Fisher's Hill, located south of Strasburg, Sheridan struck the opening blow of his 1864 Shenandoah Campaign with victory at the Third Battle of Winchester on September 19.[10] Throughout the day Sheridan's three infantry corps, followed by his cavalry, constantly pressured Early's command and forced it out of Winchester. "We drove them gradually all day and about night they commenced a hasty retreat," recalled the Twenty-ninth Maine's Ezekiel Hanson of the Union success.[11]

As the Army of the Shenandoah secured Winchester, the hopes of the town's Confederates plummeted while the town's Unionists and African Americans beamed with optimism at the prospect of being under Union rule. As troops from the Second Rhode Island Infantry entered Winchester, they spied "one brave girl, her heart still filled with love for the Union," vigorously waving "'Old Glory' between the infuriated hosts."[12] Julia Chase, one of Winchester's staunchest Unionist sympathizers, confided to her diary in the aftermath of Sheridan's victory at Winchester: "For the first time we have seen a glorious victory in the Valley of the Shenandoah on the part of our troops."[13] A soldier from a New York regiment noted the reactions of area African Americans to Sheridan's success at Winchester. "American citizens of African descent, are beginning to make their appearance" to realize the dream of emancipation—something that had been extremely tenuous for the region's African Americans until Sheridan's victories.[14]

For the veterans of Sheridan's army, especially those who had fought in previous campaigns in the Shenandoah Valley that resulted in disaster, the Union triumph at Winchester signaled a new beginning for Union operations in the region. The Twenty-ninth Maine's John Mead Gould, who had fought previously in the valley, captured the significance of this success: "I have been in the Army all the time the war has been in existence…I am happy in knowing that there is an end to all hard times and I begin to feel that my days of retreating before a victorious army are ended."[15]

In the immediate aftermath of the Union triumph at Winchester, some criticized Sheridan's decision to not immediately pursue Early's

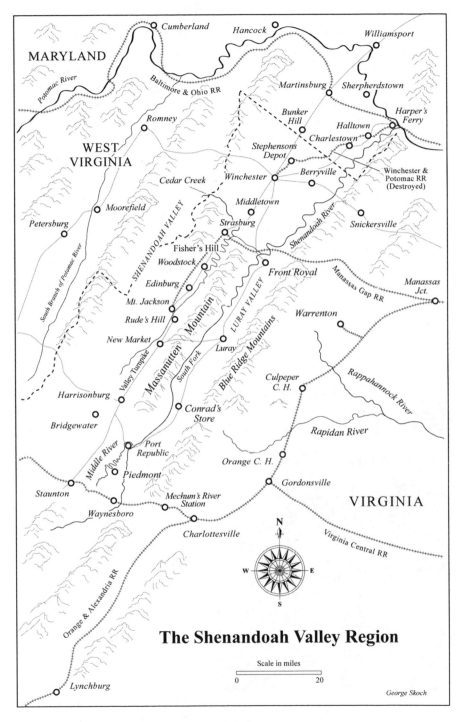

Map of the Shenandoah Valley. *Prepared by George Skoch.*

army south. Sheridan, however, realized he could not. After a full day of fighting, Sheridan believed his men needed rest before they marched south to corral Early's command. "It was not in human endurance that our infantry, after the toils of the last twenty-four hours, could follow immediately in pursuit," recalled the 114th New York's James Franklin Fitts.[16] While Sheridan's army rested that evening, he issued orders to be prepared to march south the following morning.[17]

As Sheridan made preparations for the pursuit, General Early hastened his army south on the Valley Pike. As Early's troops marched, some of the veterans of his army—so accustomed to success in the valley—seemed demoralized by the crushing blow suffered at Winchester, and some exhibited doubt as to Early's ability to lead the army to victory against Sheridan. Confederate cavalryman John Opie recalled: "What was left of our army had now lost all confidence in General Early as a leader, and they were, therefore, much demoralized."[18] Private John O. Casler, who called the Shenandoah Valley home, believed that a significant portion of Early's command had lost faith in him after Winchester. "General Early was to blame for the defeat. He displayed poor generalship," Casler observed. The disgruntled infantryman continued: "The corps never had any confidence in him afterwards."[19] General John B. Gordon, one of Early's division commanders who criticized Early's generalship during the 1864 Shenandoah Campaign perhaps more ardently than anyone else, noted that the Confederate army retreated "drearily and silently, with burdened brains and aching hearts."[20]

Despite the opinions of some Confederate soldiers, Shenandoah Valley civilians who observed Early's retreat from Winchester saw a defeated army but not a demoralized one. As Early's troops passed

General John B. Gordon. *Battles & Leaders.*

Springdale, a stately limestone structure on the east side of the Valley Pike south of Kernstown, Robert T. Barton, who had served the Confederate war effort until tuberculosis forced his discharge in October 1862, did not believe Early's command disheartened. "There was not a little confusion and disorder and many ambulances and wagons of wounded men," Barton observed, "but no panic nor any apparent apprehension that at a more advantageous place Early would turn his veterans round to confront his foes."[21]

As General Early directed his column southward, he did have one "advantageous place" in mind to reverse the fortunes of his army: Fisher's Hill. Located just south of Strasburg, Fisher's Hill marked the point where the Shenandoah Valley reached its narrowest point of 3.9 miles. Bordered by Little North Mountain on the west and Massanutten Mountain on the east, the northward-facing slope of Fisher's Hill, which is more precipitous on its eastern end, offered the Confederates, in Early's opinion, "the only place where a stand could be made."[22] Tumbling Run, a small creek that traversed the ground in front of Fisher's Hill, also afforded another obstacle to an attacking force.

General Early knew the Shenandoah Valley well and understood that if he did not attempt to make a defensive stand at Fisher's Hill, then his next-best chance for a reasonable defense would be in the upper part of the Shenandoah Valley in one of the gaps of the Blue Ridge Mountains. Although it might have been a movement to save his army, he knew that such a radical withdrawal would leave the lower Shenandoah Valley and significant portions of the upper valley open to Sheridan and allow the Union army to lay waste to the region. With all of those factors considered, Early concluded: "This was the only position in the whole Valley where a defensive line could be taken against an enemy moving up the Valley."[23]

Despite the apparently impenetrable defensive nature of Fisher's Hill, it had one significant flaw: an army could not fully realize its defensive potential if it did not have enough troops to stretch from Little North Mountain to Massanutten Mountain. Edward A. Pollard, editor of the *Richmond Examiner* and one of the architects of the postwar ideology of the Lost Cause, correctly observed this flaw: "The ground there is unsuitable to receive an attack upon, unless the force standing on the defensive is strong enough to reach from mountain to mountain."[24] That proved Early's greatest difficulty. The best estimates of the amount of Confederate troops available to defend Early's position at Fisher's Hill place the overall strength of his command between 8,000 and 8,500 men—nowhere close to the amount needed to stretch the nearly four-mile front of Fisher's Hill.[25] In addition to the small size of his army, Early had to weaken it further by sending two cavalry brigades under General Williams C. Wickham to protect the Luray Valley from Union cavalry.[26] With all the various impediments Early confronted, he attempted as best as possible to defend Fisher's Hill with his four infantry divisions and remaining cavalry (some of which was dismounted), but those efforts proved futile on September 22. The Thirteenth Virginia's captain, Samuel Buck, a Shenandoah Valley native who served in Early's army, observed the Confederate conundrum: "The position was a very strong one, but our army was too small to man it."[27]

Although heavily outnumbered, Early hoped that if he could make his position appear strong, it might deter Sheridan's efforts to attack. After all, in August 1864, during a period of maneuvering between Sheridan and Early in what one soldier referred to as a "mimic war," Early placed his forces on Fisher's Hill and dared Sheridan to attack; Sheridan did not.[28] The circumstances in late September proved different, as Sheridan already had one victory over Early and the Confederate army was approximately half the size it had been in August. Still, Early clung to hope that the memories of August would deter Sheridan.

"I determined therefore to make a show of a stand here," Early explained, "with the hope that the enemy would be deterred from attacking me in this position, as had been the case in August."[29] In spite of the obstacles, Early appeared, by some accounts, to maintain a positive spirit. For example, as he passed through Strasburg on his way to Fisher's Hill with his bedraggled army he apparently informed some of the town's civilians "that he would hold his position at Fisher's Hill against any force which the Yankees could bring against him."[30]

Another issue that hampered Early's efforts to establish a

General Jubal A. Early. *Battles & Leaders.*

suitable defense was that his officer corps had been depleted at the Third Battle of Winchester. In addition to the loss of some able regimental and brigade commanders, Early had lost arguably one of his best division commanders in General Robert E. Rodes on September 19, and even before the battle, a directive from the Confederate War Department had weakened Early's officer corps. Several days prior to Rodes's demise at Winchester, the Confederate War Department, unaware of the fate yet to fall on Early's Valley Army, ordered General John C. Breckinridge, who presided over two of Early's divisions, to return to his role as commander of the Department of Southwest Virginia.[31] By September 21, Breckinridge, one of Early's most trusted confidants and popular generals with the men in the ranks, had left Early's army to resume his old post in the southwestern corner of the Old Dominion.[32] "I lost the benefit of his services," Early wrote of Breckinridge's departure. Early continued that Breckinridge "ably co-operated with me, and our personal relations had been of the most pleasant character."[33] One of Early's staff officers noted simply: "Breckinridge...left us."[34]

By about noon on September 20, Early's army had concentrated atop Fisher's Hill and set to the task of strengthening the position that bore the grand nom de plume "Gibraltar of the Valley." Amid the task of digging in, many of Early's troops looked for an opportunity to rest. From private soldiers to generals, the Third Battle of Winchester and the hasty retreat of nearly twenty miles exacted a heavy toll on the physical condition of the soldiers. General Bryan Grimes, who commanded one of Early's brigades, wrote to his wife, Elizabeth: "I have never exerted myself so much in my life and my voice was completely gone. I was sore as a boil all over." Grimes's discomfort on September 20 became so unbearable that he had to have a servant named "Polk" rub liniment over him.[35]

In the aftermath of the Third Battle of Winchester, Sheridan's troops, although euphoric over their victories, suffered from physical exhaustion. After giving his troops the night to rest, Sheridan ordered his army to march south in pursuit of Early's army at daylight.[36] Sheridan's cavalry led the way. General James Wilson's cavalry division advanced toward Front Royal, to protect Sheridan's eastern flank while General William Averell's division rode south on the Middle Road. General Wesley Merritt's cavalry division rode south up the Valley Pike and paved the way for Sheridan's infantry and artillery. As the Union cavalry rode south, undoubtedly in an effort to further demoralize the area's Confederate civilians, it displayed many of the Confederate flags captured at the Third Battle of Winchester.[37] For much of the movement on September 20, Sheridan's cavalry encountered little opposition. Not until one

The Steele House, located on the west side of the Valley Pike in Newtown (present-day Stephens City) as it appeared in the 1880s. *Linden "Butch" Fravel/Stone House Foundation collection.*

of Merritt's brigades, commanded by Colonel Thomas Devin, reached the intersection of the Valley Pike and Cedar Creek south of Middletown did the Federals confront any resistance. Devin easily brushed the opposition aside and pushed through Strasburg to secure the town.[38]

As word reached civilians in the communities between Winchester and Strasburg of the approach of Sheridan's army, the civilians whose sympathies rested with the Confederacy performed the familiar task of securing personal property so that it did not fall into the hands of Sheridan's men. John Steele, a resident of Newtown (present-day Stephens City), who lived in a house that stood on the west side of the Valley Pike, made hurried preparations to secure his family's cherished possessions when he received word of Sheridan's advance. "All that day we were busy hiding our household effects, digging holes in the yard and garden, burying…silverware, queensware, meats, and even some clothing," he confided to his diary.[39] Although able to protect some valuables, Steele reported that Sheridan's men "stole flour and salt… [and] apples, grapes, and chickens."[40]

After the Steeles realized that all most Union soldiers wanted was food, they decided to make some apple pies and sell them to the Federal troops for fifty cents each. John Steele noted that his family made about twenty dollars. However, when the Union soldiers ate them, they found them less than delectable. In an effort to make the pies quickly, and perhaps do their part for the Confederate war effort, the Steeles used water instead of shortening to make the crust. Furthermore, they did not cook the apples, nor did the Steeles add any sugar to sweeten the pies. One Union account noted that the "pies were deleterious trash…when eaten," and the soldiers who consumed the pies were stricken with "a season of colic or similar complaints."[41]

When Sheridan arrived in Newtown, he ordered the Second United States Cavalry to detach itself from Colonel Charles Russell Lowell's brigade and serve as an escort for the general's staff as it rode the final distance to assess Early's defense at Fisher's Hill. The Second U.S.'s Theophilus Rodenbough noted that very shortly after the regiment reported to Sheridan in Newtown, the commanding general "galloped forward" with such great speed that the troopers, with their "jaded horses, vainly struggled to keep in sight of the headquarters flag."[42]

By the late afternoon of September 20, Sheridan's army had approached the environs of Strasburg. As Union troops peered south from the vicinity of Hupp's Hill, one of Sheridan's men noted, "We could see the hill lifting itself up menacingly to our advance."[43] The sight of Fisher's Hill and the occasional sound of Confederate artillery booming in the distance as Early's gunners tried to slow Sheridan's cavalry as it entered Strasburg caused angst among some in the Army of the Shenandoah and reminded them that, although they had defeated Early once, they had still not won the fight for supremacy in the Shenandoah Valley.

After General Sheridan surveyed the situation on the afternoon of the twentieth, he summoned his corps commanders to discuss the available options to break Early's defenses. As he gathered his chief lieutenants, Sheridan explained to them that one option had to be taken off the table immediately: a direct frontal assault. "A reconnaissance made pending these movements convinced me that the enemy's position at Fisher's Hill was so strong that a direct assault would entail unnecessary destruction of life," Sheridan recalled, "and besides, be of doubtful result."[44] Longtime friend and former West Point classmate General George Crook, commander of Sheridan's Eighth Corps, echoed "Little

General George Crook, commander of the Union Eighth Corps. *Library of Congress.*

Phil's" sentiments. One of Crook's staff recalled simply that the plan of a frontal assault "met with Crook's disapproval."[45]

With a frontal attack clearly not a viable option, Sheridan and his subordinates discussed the plausibility of an attack against General Early's right flank held by General Gabriel Wharton's division. General Horatio G. Wright, the commander of the Sixth Corps, and General William Emory, the commander of the Nineteenth Corps, initially favored the idea, but Crook disapproved. Crook's judgment proved sound. In addition to the fact that Sheridan's soldiers, in order to launch a successful flank attack, would have to cross the North Fork of the Shenandoah River and then attack against the steepest portion of Fisher's Hill, Crook did not believe that the movement could be executed in secrecy, as the Confederate signal station perched atop the commanding heights of Signal Knob would observe every move. Captain Henry DuPont, Crook's artillery chief, noted that from Signal Knob, the Confederates "completely overlooked Sheridan's army. This gave them full information in regard to its position and, while daylight lasted, as to every movement of the Federal troops."[46] After Sheridan digested Crook's disapproval of an attack against Early's right flank, Crook suggested that the best option lay with a flank attack against the western portion of Early's line. According to one of Crook's subordinates, Crook had "carefully" reconnoitered the area near the Back Road and Little North Mountain and suggested that he could take the Union's Eighth Corps onto the eastern face of Little North Mountain and position it so that it threatened Early's left and rear.[47]

Sheridan needed some time to mull over this option. He ordered his corps commanders to go back to their respective commands and meet again at army headquarters later that evening for a final council of war to determine the best method to strike Early's defenses.[48]

As Crook returned to his camp on the north bank of Cedar Creek, he felt confident that a surprise attack against Early's left flank offered the only opportunity for Union success. Despite his personal convictions, Crook did not believe he could sell the idea to Sheridan, Wright and Emory. Crook never seemed to hold much self-confidence in his ability to articulate ideas to those above him in rank.[49] One West Virginia officer noted of Crook's apparent insecurity: "Crook was always preeminently a man of action and found great difficulty in expressing his views in spoken words." As recognition of that deficiency, Crook brought his two division commanders, Colonels Rutherford B. Hayes and Joseph Thoburn, to the evening war council. Before the three men journeyed to the meeting, Crook explained the merits of a strike against the western end of Early's defenses. Although the terrain and keeping the flank maneuver a secret from Early still posed some challenges, both Hayes and Thoburn concurred with Crook that striking Early's western flank seemed the best available option. Hayes seemed to think, according to one West Virginia officer, that even if the flank attack did not work, the "move could result in slight loss if unsuccessful, and might produce great results if successful."[50]

When Sheridan's corps commanders met on the evening of September 20 for their final council of war, Colonel Hayes, a Harvard-trained lawyer and, as one observed noted, a "talker by profession," presented the case for the Eighth Corps to lead

Colonel Joseph Thoburn. *Nicholas P. Picerno collection.*

the flank attack against Early's left. At the "somewhat stormy council of war," Hayes made a most eloquent appeal to Sheridan to allow Crook to conduct the turning movement, just as had been done the previous day at the Third Battle of Winchester.[51] General Wright, however, would hear none of it.

Wright, senior to Crook in rank, believed that conducting the initial attack against Early's position should be his privilege, as it was "the post of honor." This statement undoubtedly enraged Crook and further weakened the bond between the two generals. Crook already held animosity against the Sixth Corps' commander for Wright's poor judgment at the Battle of Cool Spring on July 18, 1864. After the battle, Crook blamed Wright for the needless destruction of one of his divisions due to the apparent incompetence of Wright, who had refused to send troops from his own Sixth Corps to support Crook's command. "I lost some valuable men here murdered by incompetency or worse," Crook complained.[52]

Colonel Rutherford B. Hayes. *Freedom Triumphant: The Fourth Period of the War of the Rebellion, 1890.*

When Wright attempted to counsel Hayes about the Sixth Corps being given "the post of honor," Hayes lambasted the general. "It is not a question of a post of honor," Hayes lectured Wright, "the question is, how can the battle be fought and won, at the least loss of life. The success of the Union arms must not at this time be jeopardized by personal interests." Wright's reaction at the evening council of war solidified some perceptions that officers in Crook's command had of the Sixth Corps' chieftain. "Wright was a good fighter, was endowed with considerable bluster and swagger, qualities usually not found in a first class fighter," a Buckeye officer explained, "and had by association from his Potomac army campaigns a feeling quite rife in that army, to never heartily work in conjunction with other corps especially if that other corps was likely to reap the lion's share of glory."[53]

After Hayes explained to Wright that personal interests needed to be put aside for the sake of military success, Hayes reminded all present that only the Eighth Corps had the qualifications necessary to make the flank attack succeed. A significant portion of the march of nearly a dozen miles would include navigating over rocky, rugged and mountainous terrain. For much of the war, many of the troops in Crook's corps had fought in the mountains of western Virginia. Neither the Sixth nor the Nineteenth Corps had any significant experience fighting in mountainous terrain. A veteran of Crook's command noted while the "6th was a fighting machine, which went into battle like a Macedonian phalanx," the attack at Fisher's Hill would not be the traditional assault to which they were accustomed.[54] Additionally, Crook commanded ten regiments whose roots were in the mountainous regions of western Virginia.[55] One veteran noted that some of the troops in Crook's corps had spent such a significant amount of their lives in the mountainous areas of western Virginia that they "always stood sidewise, with one foot higher than the other."[56] Another recalled "that the West Virginia troops were mostly mountaineers, all of them had grown accustomed to service in the mountains, and that the move through the woods and brush along the mountain side was entirely practicable with such troops."[57]

Once the bickering stopped, Sheridan carefully weighed his options and approved the flank attack with Crook's corps to lead the assault while the troops from Wright's and Emory's corps distracted Early with a show of force all along the Confederate front. With the point of attack determined, Sheridan and his subordinates next needed to hash out the details of how the plan would be executed. First and foremost, all in the Union high command in the Shenandoah Valley understood that the plan's chance of success rested in the ability of Crook's corps to remain nearly invisible to the Confederate signal station atop Signal Knob for as long as possible. Accordingly, Sheridan ordered Crook to keep his corps concealed in a heavy body of woods on the north side of Cedar Creek the remainder of the night and not begin the march until after sunset on September 21. Crook issued orders to all of his subordinates to make certain that no one did anything to give away the corps' concealed position—not even make a fire to cook or stay warm. An understandably disgruntled veteran of the Fourteenth West Virginia recorded that after Crook's command concealed itself in the woods north of Cedar Creek, they "were not allowed to make light by night nor smoke by day."[58]

The other detail that consumed Sheridan's attention on the night of September 20 was using a portion of his cavalry to cut off Early's retreat route. To eliminate a Confederate escape path, Sheridan sent his cavalry chief, General Alfred T.A. Torbert, with two brigades from General Wesley Merritt's division to move to Front Royal. There Sheridan wanted Torbert to join with General James H. Wilson's two cavalry brigades and then move south up the Luray Valley, cross the Massanutten Mountain at New Market Gap and block Early's avenue of retreat.[59]

The medical director of the Army of the Shenandoah, surgeon James T. Ghiselin, also made preparations that evening for the impending battle. He first ordered each infantry corps to establish a field hospital in the vicinity of Strasburg and that each of the various division medical officers take necessary steps to ensure the safe evacuation of "wounded to the rear." Next, and perhaps most importantly, he pressed the generals to make certain that each soldier be given rations. Aware that the large majority of troops in the army had been without rations for twenty-four hours, Ghiselin reminded the army's generals "that no forward movement could be made until rations could be issued."[60]

That night, as Early's troops rested atop their fortified position on Fisher's Hill and Sheridan held confidence in the Union strategy, the rank and file of the Army of the Shenandoah, still unaware of the plan, pondered how they would drive Early from Fisher's Hill. An officer in Wright's corps, who recognized that "Fisher's Hill was thus always ready for rebel occupation," expressed his fear for "an order for some reckless assault."[61] Despite the confidence instilled in Sheridan's men after their victory at Winchester, the veterans of the Army of the Shenandoah—particularly those who had fought previously in the Shenandoah Valley—held tremendous respect for Early's army and knew the Confederates would not relinquish Fisher's Hill without a fight. "We had, it is true," noted the 114th New York's captain, James F. Fitts, "the prestige of victory, and the Confederates had the discouragement of defeat…but their army…was made up of veterans, and now occupied one of the best defensive positions in Virginia; and that it would be held with all the stubbornness of veterans we could not doubt."[62]

Doubt crept into the minds of Union soldiers on the night of September 20, not just because they respected the tenacity of Early's veterans, but also because Sheridan's men encountered some Confederate sympathizers in the environs around Strasburg who "laughed at the idea" of Sheridan's men successfully "taking Fisher's Hill."[63] Although some might have initially questioned the Union army's ability to capture the heights of Fisher's Hill, what countered that uncertainty was the confidence some of the soldiers in the Army of the Shenandoah had in General Sheridan. A New York officer noted: "No commander, I verily believe, ever succeeded in establishing himself so firmly in the faith of those under him as Philip H. Sheridan. He is the impersonation of victory; he looks it; he talks it."[64] The fighting over the next two days would only further solidify that New Yorker's observation.

Chapter Two

"An Unexpected Determination to Remain in Possession of It"

In the early morning dawn, about 5:00 a.m. on September 21, Sheridan's plan to crush Early's army got underway as two cavalry brigades from General Wesley Merritt's division made their way toward Front Royal as part of the Union effort to secure the Luray Valley and block any potential Confederate retreat path. While Merritt's horsemen rode east, General Averell's cavalry division moved to the small crossroads of Lebanon Church, west of Strasburg. Slightly less than three hours later, Sheridan directed Averell to move his division along the Middle Road and Back Road "until stopped by a superior force of the enemy." Averell's troopers pushed aside some token Confederate resistance along the Back Road and then rode to within sight of the left of Early's army ensconced atop Fisher's Hill. After a quick inspection of the Confederate position, Averell reported a "strong line" of Confederates and informed Sheridan "that cavalry could not carry the position without co-operative movements of infantry…hugging the base of the North Mountain."[65]

While the Union cavalry inaugurated Union movements on the morning of the twenty-first, "when the mists of early dawn cleared away," Sheridan and General Wright reconnoitered Early's position.[66] After that reconnaissance, Sheridan believed it best to move his army, sans Crook's corps, closer to the Confederate position. At some point prior to noon, when Sheridan maneuvered his troops, he ordered regimental officers to read the notes of congratulations sent to the army by President Lincoln, Secretary Stanton and General Grant, undoubtedly in an effort to instill confidence

Eng^d by A.H. Ritchie.

General Horatio Wright, commander of the Union Sixth Corps. *Author's collection.*

in his men as they moved nearer to the daunting heights of Fisher's Hill.[67] The message of gratitude from Stanton also informed Sheridan of his appointment as brigadier general in the regular army. After the soldiers in Sheridan's army listened to the brief remarks and learned that multiple one-hundred-gun salutes had been fired in their honor, the Sixth and Nineteenth Corps began their march around Strasburg.[68]

As Wright's and Emory's corps moved south, Confederate soldiers, busily "fixing" their defensive line atop Fisher's Hill, took notice of the Union advance.[69] A Louisiana officer recalled seeing "great clouds of dust hanging over the…pike, indicating the advance of the enemy…an animating spectacle it was…their arms glistening in the sun."[70]

After several hours, Wright's corps cleared Strasburg. Once Wright's infantry moved beyond Strasburg's southern boundary, they encountered

Modern-day view from the vicinity of Flint Hill looking south toward the main Confederate line. *Photograph by author.*

Confederate skirmishers posted on a series of undulating rises between the ground southwest of Strasburg and the main Confederate line atop Fisher's Hill. Not to be slowed by Early's pickets, Sheridan ordered Captain William H. McCartney's Battery A, First Massachusetts Artillery, to the right of Wright's Sixth Corps—located on a piece of high ground on the west side of the Manassas Gap Railroad—to clear the pickets and weaken the section of the Confederate line defended by General John Pegram's division. When the guns opened fire, sketch artist James Taylor "could feel the vibration of the shells in their fight." Confederate batteries responded to McCartney's guns.[71] While McCartney's cannons lobbed fifty-seven shells at their foe, Sheridan and Wright surveyed the terrain to the south and the west. As Sheridan peered to the west, he noted that a body of Confederate soldiers still held a piece of high ground known locally as Flint Hill.[72] Sheridan at once directed Wright to occupy it.[73]

As the highest elevation between Early's position and the Union line Sheridan knew that if his army occupied Flint Hill, it would not only serve as an advantageous artillery position but would also give him "an unobstructed view of the enemy's works." Confederate forces also understood the value of Flint Hill. While Early's pickets might have had no problem relinquishing other pieces of high ground on the north side of Tumbling Run, his defenders on Flint Hill refused to budge. A Vermonter in Wright's corps recalled: "The enemy, aware of its value to us, had occupied it, and instead of leaving it when they abandoned the remainder of the hither side of the stream, they evinced an unexpected determination to remain in possession of it."[74]

About 5:00 p.m., several companies of the 139th Pennsylvania advanced against the Confederate skirmishers from Pegram's and Ramseur's divisions on Flint Hill, but according to their brigade commander, Colonel James Warner, they were promptly "repulsed."[75] As the Pennsylvanians engaged Confederate skirmishers, Colonel Joseph Warren Keifer moved his brigade into position behind the right flank of the Sixth Corps. Keifer, who had been informed by his division commander, General James Ricketts, that he would more than likely "not…be engaged in the coming battle," was in the process of telling his men about "the prospect for freedom from severe work the coming day" when General Ricketts summoned Keifer to send one regiment to support the beleaguered 139th Pennsylvania.[76]

Colonel Joseph Warren Keifer. *Library of Congress.*

Keifer responded to Ricketts's order and sent Captain George W. Hoge's 126th Ohio to support the troops from the Keystone State. The Ohioans, a considerable number of whom were "inexperienced soldiers" as new recruits, marched forward. Confederate marksmen from Pegram's and Ramseur's divisions, from the protection of their bullpens (U-shaped barricades made of fence rails which protected three men) on Flint Hill, delivered "a galling fire" into Hoge's regiment.[77]

As Keifer watched the 126th Ohio give way and spied some of the Confederates abandon their bullpens to give chase to the Ohioans, he ordered Captain Clifton K. Prentiss's Sixth Maryland to stem the tide.[78] Prentiss's regiment, although "successful in driving the enemy" back to their bullpens, could not entirely dislodge them from Flint Hill. About 6:00 p.m., nearly one hour after the first attempt to occupy Flint Hill, General Wright determined to apply more consistent pressure to drive Ramseur's and Pegram's skirmishers from the heights. Wright turned to Colonel James M. Warner's brigade of Pennsylvanians and New Yorkers. With bayonets fixed, Warner's regiments surged forward and finally carried the position.[79] A newspaper correspondent noted simply that the attack of Warner's brigade "was done in splendid style."[80] When the Union regiments finally seized the heights, they let out a collective cheer that wafted through the air. Troops from Sheridan's army who had not been involved in the struggle for Flint Hill celebrated the success of Warner's command and "re-echoed the shouts of triumph."[81]

After Warner's regiments secured Flint Hill, Wright's entire Sixth Corps moved forward to occupy the ground—a task that, in itself, contained a number of challenges. By the time Warner's brigade captured Flint Hill, the sun had begun to set, meaning much of the Sixth Corps' march took place in the darkness over extremely rugged terrain. "Having secured this commanding point," General Wright explained, "the corps was at once moved forward and to the right to occupy it, a movement which in the darkness, and owing to the darkness of the ground, cut up by ravines and covered by dense woods, took nearly all night to accomplish."[82]

Following the arduous fight for Flint Hill, General Wright shifted his divisions to the west to occupy the commanding ground. The movement, which took the better part of the night of the twenty-first to complete, placed the Sixth Corps in a semicircular line that followed the contours of Flint Hill. While the divisions of Generals George Getty and Frank Wheaton joined Ricketts's division on Flint Hill, the Sixth Corps' pioneers used their axes to clear trees for Union artillery. As the infantry arrived throughout the night and took its place in line, there was little time for rest as it was, but they were also ordered to dig in and make the already advantageous position even stronger.[83] A Vermont officer in the Sixth Corps noted of the night's work after Wright's veterans formed on Flint Hill: "Entrenching tools were soon brought forward, and the night wore toilsomely away."[84]

On the other flank of Sheridan's army, as the elements of the Sixth Corps attacked and secured Flint Hill, Sheridan ordered General Emory to do two things. First, he directed Emory to "ascertain the force of the enemy that was across the Shenandoah River."[85] Emory ordered Colonel Thomas

General William Emory, commander of the Union Nineteenth Corps. *Author's collection.*

W. Cahill's Ninth Connecticut across one of the Shenandoah's fords with orders to "feel the enemy's position."[86] Cahill took two companies and crossed. However, the Confederate cavalry that defended Early's extreme right flank charged into Cahill's infantry and forced them to the river's north bank.[87] Second, Sheridan ordered Emory to "hold the road leading to Front Royal" from Strasburg.[88] Sheridan knew that if any attempt would be made to reinforce Early's army, then that body of troops would more than likely come from the direction of Front Royal. To carry out this directive, Emory turned to the 114th New York.

As the sun began to set, the 114th New York "marched through the dingy, dilapidated village of Strasburg, and…the men were posted to the banks of the Shenandoah River."[89]

As the New Yorkers rested along the picket line, the "quietude" of the "pleasant night" was suddenly interrupted "by a burst of instrumental music." Some of the officers in the 114th New York, including Captain James Fitts, believed it might be the signal of an attack. "It was, I presume, the headquarters band of one of the Confederate generals, on their extreme right…I judged it to be very near," Fitts explained, "and sent out immediately to warn the pickets to increased vigilance." The music, which proved to be more than a mile away and portended no threat, ultimately offered a tranquil moment as the soldiers of both sides prepared for the impending battle. Fitts noted that after the Confederate band played "Dixie," they then regaled their Union counterparts with "John Brown" and "Yankee Doodle."[90]

While the sound of the Confederate band wafted through the evening air, the Confederate civilians of Strasburg fretted for their safety and the well-being of Early's army. When artist-correspondent James Taylor encountered Henry Keister, a potter, Taylor noted that the "gentleman seemed somewhat dazed by the demoralized situation of affairs." When Taylor inquired as to whether or not Keister would allow him to board at his home (located at the northwest corner of the intersection of the Valley Pike and Main Street) for the night, Keister initially refused. Understandably, Keister feared it might be a ploy by Union soldiers to seize his property. Taylor explained to Keister that the best protection his property could receive was allowing an artist-correspondent attached to the Union army to stay at his house. "I fully appreciated and excused his reluctance to accommodate me," Taylor remarked, "but won him over with the plausible argument that one of my profession quartered on him would serve as a wholesome check to impositions of thieving stragglers."[91]

Although Keister's initial fears were temporarily allayed, they returned about 8:00 p.m., when Union soldiers from General William Emory's Nineteenth Corps climbed onto Keister's back porch and demanded "the blood of the spy." When Taylor heard the clamor outside, he peered out the window and concluded that "some poor devil's in for it." Soon a loud knock at Taylor's door startled him. Union soldiers threw the door open, seized Taylor and called immediately to "Hang the Rebel spy!" Mr. Keister, believing he had inadvertently been harboring a Confederate spy, feared for his life. The contingent of Union soldiers arrested Taylor, but only one escorted him to the headquarters of General William Dwight, commander of Emory's first division. After Dwight examined Taylor's pass, he expressed his regret and allowed Taylor to return to Mr. Keister's residence, escorted by the same Union soldier who had taken Taylor to Dwight.[92]

Although inconvenient for Taylor and Keister, Taylor's arrest exemplified Sheridan's desire to maintain strict security on the night of September 21 as Crook's Eighth Corps—which had been concealed on the north bank of Cedar Creek—marched south toward Hupp's Hill to a position where Crook concealed his two divisions "in a clump of timber" behind the hill.[93] The night march, which covered approximately five miles, left some of Crook's men in a surly mood. Not fully understanding the overall plan, a soldier in the Fourteenth West Virginia, Jesse Tyler Sturm, believed that Crook's corps "wandered around all night, doing nothing and getting nowhere...the men were all in bad humor indeed."[94]

Not all of Crook's troops saw things as pessimistically that evening as Sturm did. A soldier in the Thirty-fourth Massachusetts noted that, while some of his comrades grumbled about staying idle for so long, marching at night and not being allowed to have a fire to cook, the veteran troops of Crook's corps coped. "Troops in the field are a jolly set of fellows, when well disciplined, well fought, and well fed," recalled the veteran from Massachusetts after the conflict, "and the spirit and humor they exhibit under adverse circumstances, and frequently even in the battle is truly wonderful."[95]

While Crook's troops navigated through the darkness on the night of the twenty-first and the veterans of Wright's command strengthened Flint Hill, General Early contemplated the meaning of the activity of that day—particularly the capture of Flint Hill. Still trusting in his army's ability to hold Fisher's Hill against "any force the Yankees could bring against him," General Early believed Sheridan would not press any farther than Flint Hill.[96] Early explained that after Wright's troops occupied Flint Hill, he "began to think he [Sheridan] was satisfied with the advantage he had gained and would not probably press it further." Early's estimation of Sheridan's intentions proved naïve.[97]

Chapter Three

"Like an Avalanche of Howling Demons"

During the night of September 21, Sheridan sent an order to Emory that required him to move the Nineteenth Corps "at the break of day [September 22] to occupy the position occupied the night before by the VI Corps, and to keep closed on the VI Corps, which was to move to the right."[98] To carry out Sheridan's order, Emory ordered reveille blown in his camps at 3:00 a.m.[99] Emory turned to General William Dwight, commander of the corps' first division, to lead the movement. Although Dwight had orders to not make the movement until "daylight," a discussion Dwight had with General Frank Wheaton, commander of the first division of Wright's corps, compelled him to alter the plan slightly and without his immediate superior's knowledge. As the commander of the division on the left of the Sixth Corps, Wheaton wanted to make certain that Dwight's command maintained a strong connection with the Sixth so that there would be no gap between Wright's and Emory's commands. Wheaton informed Dwight that his division would make its final shift to the west "before daylight" and that Dwight "must follow his division to connect." Dwight believed, in his capacity as a division commander, he had some latitude in the execution of his order so long as he took into consideration the best interests of the army. "I considered this a proper execution of the order," Dwight explained.[100]

While Dwight might have been correct to move his division about half an hour before daybreak, he did not supervise the move directly. Since Dwight viewed the maneuver as "neither a difficult nor a hazardous one," he left the

General William F. Dwight. *Nicholas P. Picerno collection.*

execution up to his staff officers and two brigade commanders, Colonel George Beal and General James McMillan.[101]

News of Dwight's shift undoubtedly enraged Emory, but his indignation rose to new heights when he rode out to check on the movement's progress and found Dwight "absent." Furthermore, Emory seethed with rage that Dwight's regiments, although they maintained their connection with Wheaton's division, did not retain their connection with the only other division in the Nineteenth Corps, General Cuvier Grover's. When Emory rode into this gap, he came under fire from "the enemy's sharpshooters" as he "rode upon the ground." Emory immediately shifted two brigades from Grover's division to cover the void in the corps' line.[102]

Afterward, the troops from Beal's and McMillan's brigades "fell to work at once entrenching."[103] Although these veterans understood the necessity of constructing earthworks once they got into their new position, the work proved difficult as the troops in those brigades had little to eat over the previous several days. A veteran of the Twenty-ninth Maine noted that his regiment "did good service with the axes and shovels which were furnished us, and before daylight we had a very substantial line of intrenchments [sic] along the brigade front. Such work is not the pleasantest on empty stomachs." Despite that hardship, the presence of the enemy and an unceasing admiration for Sheridan compelled the men to summon the strength to perform the task with little complaint. "Men will always readily build breastworks in presence of the enemy," noted an officer in Beal's brigade, "besides, we knew that Sheridan had ordered them, and that hence it was all right."[104]

The sound of the Union axes and shovels wafted through the early morning air and caught the attention of Confederate pickets. As dawn approached, Confederate infantry opened fire on Dwight's soldiers as they attempted to entrench. While too dark to see, Early's pickets aimed in the direction of the sounds coming from the Union lines. An officer in Beal's brigade recalled of this early morning Confederate musket fire: "At dawn of day the bullets began to whistle over us, fired by the rebel pickets who aimed only at the sounds."[105]

While most of the soldiers in Emory's corps focused on the task of strengthening their defensive positions, a soldier from the 114th New York decided to forage for something to eat. This unnamed soldier, identified by a regimental officer as "a vagrant…one of the class of bummers who are nothing if continually eating and drinking," commandeered a beehive to share with his fellow comrades. The New Yorker brought "it triumphantly" back to the regiment, but just as he reached the line of the 114th New York, a bee flew out of the hive and stung him in the neck. This compelled the "vagrant soldier" to drop the hive. When the hive hit the ground, the bees inside flew out and attacked the New Yorkers. Captain James Fitts, whose face was stung four times by the bees, recorded of the comedic episode: "It proved a perfect Pandoras Box of ills to my little command…All over the field, the unhappy soldiers were rolling and twisting in the grass; the air resounded with their laughter and expletives." Some of the men even jovially surmised that these bees might have held strong Confederate sympathies as, when the New Yorkers regained their composure, they noticed that the bees had formed a perfect swarm over the regimental stacks of arms, precluding the veterans of the 114th access to their muskets. "The bees settled in a great, angry cloud directly above the stacked arms," noted a veteran of the regiment, "as if to forbid our resuming them."[106]

As the New Yorkers dealt with the anxieties of being attacked by angry bees, the inhabitants of Strasburg experienced different fears as the opening salvos from Confederate pickets shredded the crisp morning air. "Every soul within the region of Strasburg was astir," noted an observer, "as the first streaks of dawn shot lavender and pink across the horizon, for the possession of Fisher's Hill was inaugurated." Artist-correspondent James Taylor awoke in the Keister household that morning to find the women of the household "paralyzed with fear" at the prospect of the impending battle.[107] When members of the Fisher household—whose home and gristmill sat at the base of Fisher's Hill and, therefore, between the lines of both armies—heard the opening shots reverberate, anxiety gripped Mrs. Fisher. Supplication to God now seemed to be her only refuge from the impending battle, as she "knelt beside the bed, her face buried in her hands, her pale lips moving in prayer."[108]

While Strasburg's citizens prepared for the worst-case scenario, so, too, did General Emory. Despite the necessity of the shifts of Dwight's division and half of Grover's division, Emory grew extremely concerned about the ability of his corps to maintain a strong connection with Wright's and also adequately protect Sheridan's left flank. Although the army's left rested on the North Fork of the Shenandoah River, Emory believed that the Shenandoah was "fordable nearly everywhere." Emory feared that at any moment Colonel Milton Ferguson's brigade of Virginia cavalry could splash across and strike the army's left.[109] While the North Fork of the Shenandoah River had a number of points where it could be forded in an attempt to turn Sheridan's left flank, Emory's assertion that it could be forded "everywhere" is probably an exaggeration, as weather records indicate that, despite a somewhat dry summer in the valley, there was consistent rainfall in the latter part of August and much of September.[110]

Although Emory's line was "much attenuated," he took every precaution in order to execute his corps' responsibilities. Emory leaned heavily on one of his brigade commanders, Colonel Edward Molineux, to secure the army's left flank and protect the "line of communication with Strasburg."[111] "Old Brick Top," as Emory was affectionately known by his men, gave Molineux command of what essentially amounted to a provisional division. The command consisted of Molineux's brigade of six regiments and Colonel Daniel Macauley's brigade of five regiments.

Molineux took every precaution to secure his left. Troops from both his and Macauley's brigades erected temporary "works" to fortify the position. He even ordered two companies of the Twenty-second Iowa to occupy Spengler's

Colonel Edward Molineux. *Fred Molineux collection.*

42

Modern-day view of Spengler's Mill (sometimes also identified as Spangler's Mill).
Photograph by author.

Mill "on the Shenandoah to guard against any advance in that direction."
Confederate sharpshooters complicated Molineux's task, as fire from their
rifles "annoyed" Union troops while they constructed their defenses.[112]

As Emory's regiments prepared their positions during the early morning
hours of September 22, Crook's command—the crucial piece to any chance
of Union success that day—prepared to move once again. After their night
march to the area just north of Hupp's Hill, Crook's men rested for several
hours, and then, around daylight, Sheridan ordered Crook to move his two
divisions "under cover of the intervening woods and ravines" to an area to
the right and rear of Wright's Sixth Corps. From this position they could get
much closer to Little North Mountain, the point from which Crook would
ultimately launch his flank assault.[113]

The movement to the west greatly concerned Crook. For the
previous two days, Crook had been able to conceal his command—the
quintessential component to Union success. Crook knew that, as he moved
his regiments closer to the front, he ran the risk of being observed by
Confederate signalman atop the commanding eminence of Massanutten

Modern-day view of Signal Knob from vicinity of Back Road near St. Stephen's Church. *Photograph by author.*

Mountain, known locally as Signal Knob. Crook, who "led the way in person" and wore the jacket of an infantry private void of his rank as a general, kept a close eye on the Confederate perch. He ordered his men to be careful to not do anything that might draw the attention of those who occupied the enemy signal station. He even directed the regimental color bearers to "trail their flags" so that the colorful banners would not give away their movement.[114]

At some point during the morning, more than likely after Crook completed his march to an area to the right and rear of Wright's command, Sheridan gathered his corps commanders atop Flint Hill in the vicinity of the Vermont Brigade to assess the strength of the Confederate position. Through a telescope mounted on a tripod, Sheridan could clearly see how Early's troops improved their position. One observer noted that Sheridan seemed to peer through the telescope for hours, "sweeping with his glass to the right and the left, evidently bent on understanding precisely the task before him; occasionally pausing to remark to some by-stander, or to mutter to himself, 'I'll get a twist on 'em, d[am]n 'em!'"[115]

Sheridan's veterans did not need a telescope to see the strength of the Confederate defenses on the morning of the twenty-second—they appeared almost impenetrable to the naked eye. Aldace Walker, an officer in the Vermont Brigade, noted of the somewhat imposing scene: "The rebels were in plain view before us…occupying a long entrenchment…with abattis in its front." Walker also noted that the Confederates continued to work "diligently" throughout the morning of September 22 with their shovels.[116]

As the morning came to a close, Sheridan determined to use his army, save Crook's command, to distract Early from the true intent of Union plans. Sheridan wanted to deceive Early and make him believe that the Union army might strike either against the Confederate right flank or make a direct frontal assault. At about 11:30 a.m., General Emory "received an intimation" from General Sheridan "to press the enemy, to mask an attack on their left."[117]

Although Sheridan did not provide any specific instructions to Emory about how "to press the enemy," Emory knew precisely what to do not only to distract the Confederates but also to better protect the Army of the Shenandoah's left flank. At some point during the late morning, presumably before Sheridan's order, Emory had ordered thirty men from Colonel George Beal's brigade to reconnoiter a piece of high ground that sat between the main Confederate stronghold of Fisher's Hill and Emory's position. The contingent of "sharpshooters," as one soldier in the brigade identified them, was ordered "to crawl out as far as [it] could go and report all [it] saw." By most accounts, the majority of those thirty soldiers from Beal's brigade did not go beyond the Union picket line. When they returned to the main Union line, they reported that "no enemy was visible, except those in the [bull] pens, and the main line nearly a mile beyond, on Fisher's Hill."[118] This information might have come as a surprise to General Emory, who had observed the enemy position throughout the day from afar and believed that Early's command had a strong line of works about four hundred yards in front of the Nineteenth Corps that extended "from the river to our right… strongly barricaded and strongly manned."[119]

In an effort to carry out his task, Emory ordered a section of Battery D, 1st Rhode Island Light Artillery, "to the left unseen by the enemy, and ordered them to enfilade the rifle-pits and shell them vigorously for twenty minutes."[120] Emory recalled that the impact of fire from these two cannons "was perfect."[121] After twenty minutes, the artillery fire ceased, and Emory ordered the infantry to assault the bullpens. Two regiments from Grover's division, the 128th New York and 176th New York, and two from Dwight's division, the 116th New York and four companies of the 30th Massachusetts, made the attack.

The defenders of those bullpens put up little resistance and took to their heels quickly for the main Confederate line. "In a gallant style they advanced on a double-quick and drove the rebs from their rifle-pits on the summit," recalled a veteran of the 128th New York.[122] An officer of the 29th Maine, who observed the attack of the 116th New York and 30th Massachusetts against the bullpens, wrote: "The charge our boys made was very successful. The rebels left, running like sheep as hard as they could go."[123] After the troops from New York and Massachusetts seized the Confederate bullpens, the Union troops immediately went to work "with spade and pick" on reversing them and strengthening the position.[124]

After the capture of the Confederate bullpens on Early's right, troops from Emory's command maintained constant pressure on that portion of Early's line throughout the afternoon in an effort to continue Sheridan's tactics of deception. The intensity of the action varied along the eastern portion of Sheridan's line.

For example, during the afternoon, Captain William H. McCartney's Battery A, First Massachusetts Artillery, positioned near the eastern fringe of Strasburg, engaged in a furious duel with Confederate artillery and cavalry commanded by Colonel Milton Ferguson. During the duel, McCartney's gunners targeted a barn owned by the Newell family when they spied Confederate sharpshooters using it for cover. Artist-correspondent James Taylor, from his perch near Banks's Fort, observed that, with a perfectly aimed shot, the barn was "reduced…to ashes" and sent "the grayjackets issuing from the building" very rapidly. On the east side of the Valley Pike, McCartney's artillery struck the Hammond family barn and set it ablaze. Taylor recalled that as the smoke from Hammond's barn billowed into the air, it seemed "demon-inspired."[125]

While McCartney's battery exchanged fire with the enemy, some of Emory's infantry fired toward the south but received no response from Confederate soldiers because there were actually none opposite them. For instance, when Captain John W. DeForest received orders to take a contingent of the Twelfth Connecticut, posted on the far left of the Union line overlooking the North Fork of the Shenandoah River, and open fire on the woods to his front, he was baffled, as it did not seem to him that any enemy force stood on the opposite bank. "It seemed ridiculous," DeForest explained, "for we could not discern a living creature over there." For several hours the troops from Connecticut unleashed their volleys at the opposite bank and received, in DeForest's estimation, no more than a total of three shots in return. At one point during the apparently senseless exercise of wasting ammunition, DeForest heard someone shout from the opposite bank of the river: "Wh—at the hell are your shoot—ing at?" The Connecticut troops stopped their fire for a moment and began to laugh. At that moment, DeForest determined the endeavor pointless and ordered his men to stop firing.[126]

Within moments after he gave the order to cease firing, one of Sheridan's staff officers rode over to the left and inquired as to why DeForest's detachment stopped shooting. DeForest informed the aide that he stopped because there were no Confederates on the opposite bank and that it was a "waste of ammunition." The officer looked jovially at DeForest and told him: "Never mind...Waste all you've got. General Sheridan wants you to keep up a tip-top racket. Blaze away as though you meant to follow up with a charge."[127] DeForest obliged Sheridan's directive and kept up a rapid fire throughout the afternoon, firing an estimated four thousand rounds. Although DeForest joked that the "squirrels and stray pigs over there must have wondered what we had against them," he fully understood after the meeting with a member of Sheridan's staff that the seemingly pointless waste of ammunition served the valuable purpose of "distracting the attention of the Southerners from our serious turning movement."[128]

As the fight against the "squirrels and stray pigs" commenced on the far left of Sheridan's line, a more serious engagement developed on the right of Emory's corps as troops from the Union Sixth Corps attempted to dislodge Confederate pickets from the bullpens in front of them. Around noon, as Emory began his push to take the bullpens to his front, General Wright received orders to march General Ricketts's division toward the Back Road and then strike the bullpens manned by troops from Ramseur's division.[129] Sheridan ordered Averell's cavalry division, already on the Back Road, to support Ricketts's movement. Colonel Joseph Warren Keifer, who commanded the second brigade in Ricketts's division, noted that, around noon, the forces of Ricketts and Averell were "rather defiantly displayed and moved conspicuously to our right, and close upon the enemy's front."[130]

Keifer sent two of his regiments—the 110th and 122nd Ohio—to attack the enemy bullpens that sat on the rise of high ground on the north side of Tumbling Run. Ramseur's defenders who manned them put up stiff resistance to the Ohioans' attack. Keifer recalled of the Confederate effort: "The enemy fought hard to hold possession of this ridge as a protection to his left and as a good lookout."[131] To Confederate soldiers on the main section

Modern-day view looking north from Ramseur's Hill toward the bullpen site defended by troops from Ramseur's division. *Photograph by author.*

of Fisher's Hill, the defense of the bullpens by Ramseur's marksmen was inspiring. The stout resistance amazed Private John H. Lane, an artillerist in Captain John L. Massie's Fluvanna Battery. "They manfully held their ground," Lane recalled of the Confederate defenders. The veterans of Ramseur's infantry who manned the main Confederate line tried to offer a psychological boost to the bullpens' defenders by filling the air with cheers of encouragement. Lane wrote of the effort: "The wild yell that went up from our lines must have made that little band of Spartans feel good."[132]

The Confederate defenders attempted to stymie the attack of the two Ohio regiments by using a branch of Tumbling Run that ran north to strike a blow against the left of Keifer's line. Keifer observed this maneuver and immediately rushed Captain Clifton Prentiss's Sixth Maryland Infantry to drive the enemy from the ravine. "In this movement I was entirely successful in driving the enemy," Prentiss reported after the battle.[133] Keifer's two Ohio regiments followed up Prentiss's success. After "repeated charges," Keifer's troops pushed Ramseur's men from their bullpens, back across Tumbling Run and into the main line of Confederate earthworks.[134] From

Private Lane's perch atop Ramseur's Hill, he noted the withdrawal from the stubbornly contested bullpens: "Another heavy line of battle was thrown against them and the poor fellows had to give way and run half a mile to get inside our lines...Many of them never lived to reached the line and of those who did not a few were wounded."[135]

After Keifer successfully secured the rise of high ground on the north side of Tumbling Run, Ricketts formed his line obliquely from north to southwest. Keifer's successful attack and later positioning of Ricketts's line "caused a great commotion among the rebels who…expected an immediate assault." What created additional fear among the Confederates on the left flank was the presence of Averell's division, which took position on a knoll behind Ricketts's brigades. An officer in Getty's division who watched the events unfold that afternoon recorded that Averell's division "ostentatiously picketed their horses on the very summit of a bare knoll on Ricketts' right and rear, as any soldier would infer, for the purpose of covering the outside of the army."[136]

As General Early watched the day unfold on September 22, he began to second guess his decision to remain at Fisher's Hill. In the aftermath of the battle—a fight in which Early's army would be routed by Sheridan's command—Early informed General Lee that on the afternoon of the twenty-second, he discovered that his position could be flanked and that he held little confidence that his "very thin" line would be able to withstand any assault. Consequently, Early stated that he ordered his command to "retire, after dark."[137] Although he did begin preparations that afternoon to withdraw, Early would not have the opportunity.

While Early contemplated withdrawal and the bulk of Sheridan's army demonstrated against the entire Confederate line, Crook's corps made their way toward the Back Road. About 2:00 p.m., Sheridan issued Crook final orders to march the Eighth Corps "still unobserved, to the eastern slope of North Mountain, and to pass around the enemy's extreme left and get on his flank and rear and drive him from his works."[138] As Crook's command traversed the ground toward Little North Mountain, troops from Wright's Sixth Corps noted that they could occasionally see "through the trees behind" them the "glimpses of the shining musket barrels of Crook's command."[139]

Approximately one hour after Sheridan issued his final directive to Crook, the men of the Eighth Corps reached the Back Road at St. Stephen's Church. When Crook reached that point, he conferred with General Averell. Crook asked Averell if he would lend one of his cavalry brigades to support the infantry assault and use his remaining cavalry brigade to prevent enemy guerrillas from

Modern-day view of St. Stephen's Church with Little North Mountain in the background. *Photograph by author.*

targeting "Crook's rear, picking up his stragglers."[140] After the brief meeting near St. Stephen's Church, Crook marched his men through a ravine into a body of woods and gave orders, as Colonel Thomas F. Wildes of the 116th Ohio recalled, to throw down and pile "up our knapsacks" and arrange "canteens and bayonet scabbards so that no noise would be made by them." With that task accomplished, Crook's command, "in the lightest kind of marching order, started up the steep, thickly wooded side of Little North Mountain. Some Union accounts state that Crook's "mountain-creepers" ascended the slope of Little North Mountain for nearly a half mile before the infantry column turned left, or south, to position itself for the assault against Early's left flank.[141]

The movement on the precipitous slopes of Little North Mountain did not come without its own set of challenges. Some of Crook's infantry lost their footing as they "moved along the jagged mountain side." A veteran of the Thirty-fourth Massachusetts recalled that many of the men were "clinging to the stunted trees and brushwood" in order to maintain their footing.[142]

As Crook's infantry navigated the uneven terrain, some of the men in Early's command apparently spied them on Little North Mountain. Private

Henry Robinson Berkeley, an artillerist in Kirkpatrick's Virginia Battery, noted in his diary for the twenty-second: "The Yanks have been moving heavy columns of infantry to their right...We can see them plainly climbing up the side of North Mountain."[143]

General Bryan Grimes could also clearly see the movement on Little North Mountain. Grimes, a brigade commander in Ramseur's division, wrote to his wife four days after the battle that, about 3:00 p.m., he "perceived two columns moving up the side of the mountain to our left." After seeing this, Grimes immediately went

General Bryan Grimes. *North Carolina Collection, University of North Carolina at Chapel Hill.*

to Ramseur and petitioned his division commander "to send a brigade or two" over to assist Lomax's cavalry division. Grimes held little faith in Lomax's troopers and believed that, if left unsupported, the Confederate "cavalry would run if attacked." When Grimes took this information to Ramseur, the division commander initially balked at the idea of Union infantry on Little North Mountain.[144]

Shortly after Grimes informed Ramseur of the movement, some of the men in the ranks also called it to Ramseur's attention. An artillerist in the Fluvanna Artillery noted that, as Ramseur passed in front of the guns, "one member of our battery called [Ramseur's] attention to what seemed to be a column of men moving on the side of North Mountain." Ramseur reacted initially by stating that "it was nothing more than a fence row." However, after Ramseur looked at Little North Mountain through his field glasses, he clearly discerned Union infantry on Little North Mountain. "My God! Two lines of the enemy's infantry," Ramseur exclaimed as he peered through his binoculars.[145]

General Stephen D. Ramseur. *Battles & Leaders.*

Now with confirmation, Grimes aggressively pushed Ramseur to send infantry to support Lomax's command, but Ramseur refused. Grimes recalled that Ramseur "declined" to send any support to Lomax "until he could communicate with General Early." Ramseur's refusal to take immediate action and obey the chain of command troubled Grimes tremendously. Grimes explained his concern to his wife four days after the battle: "My anxiety for the fate of the army was intolerable."[146]

Although Grimes could do little to persuade Ramseur to take immediate action, he believed he could do something to protect his brigade, which stood on the division's western flank. Grimes moved three of his regiments—the Thirty-second and Forty-fifth North Carolina regiments and the Second North Carolina battalion—into position to protect against an assault from the west while the Forty-third and Fifty-third North Carolina remained facing to the north.[147]

As Grimes prepared for the attack, soldiers in the ranks wondered why more was not being done to guard against this seemingly imminent threat. "Private soldiers began to look around and to examine with a critical eye our means, or rather our want of means, of defence," noted Private Lane. The artillerist continued in condemnation: "Gen. Ramseur...did not seem to anticipate any flank movement of the enemy...No disposition that I could see was made to meet this flank movement," recalled the Confederate artillerist.[148]

Despite the harsh criticism of the likes of Private Lane, who believed that Ramseur lacked the "qualities which could estimate the numbers or penetrate the designs of the enemy," Ramseur was not totally oblivious to the potential of an assault against Early's western flank. Ramseur knew that the nature of the terrain and a thinly manned line invited attack.[149] Captain

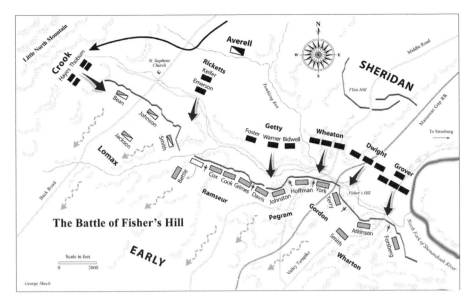

Map of troop positions during the Battle of Fisher's Hill. *Map prepared by George Skoch.*

James M. Garnett, an ordnance officer in the division, noted that both Lomax and Ramseur anticipated an attack and never expected to be able to successfully resist it. Two days after the battle, Garnett wrote: "Both General Lomax, who commanded the cavalry, and General Ramseur, considered that, if an attack was made against our left (which was very probable), it was very questionable whether it would be repulsed."[150]

Regardless of the fact that Ramseur might have anticipated a Union strike from the west, he still felt compelled to seek Early's counsel and respect the chain of command. With the presence of Ricketts's division to his front, Ramseur might have feared that a unilateral decision to redeploy his troops would inaugurate a premature Union attack and eliminate any chances for a successful Confederate withdrawal that night.

Unfortunately for the Confederates who defended Fisher's Hill, no significant repositioning of troops by General Early ever occurred to meet the impending danger from Little North Mountain. The question of why Early did not react remains today. No Confederate sources clearly indicate Early's location on the afternoon of September 22 or if Ramseur's communications ever reached Early. More than likely—since Early had nothing to gain but eternal embarrassment from ignoring communications from Ramseur—Ramseur's message did not reach him before the flank attack commenced.[151]

The worst fears of the Confederates on Early's left flank started to be realized about 4:00 p.m., as Crook's two divisions faced east and moved down the slopes of Little North Mountain toward Lomax's cavalry. According to Crook, approximately two hundred yards before he was going to give the order for his divisions to march by the left flank and thus face east, they encountered Confederate skirmishers from the Eighth Virginia Cavalry. As the sound of small arms fire rolled into the main Confederate line, Rebel gunners lobbed artillery shells against Little North Mountain. It had little effect. "We had encountered the skirmishers of the enemy some 200 yards before facing by the left flank," Crook recalled approximately one month after the battle. He continued: "As soon as we were discovered, they opened on the woods with artillery, doing but little execution."[152]

After Crook's men brushed aside the elements of the 8th Virginia Cavalry—with Hayes's division on the right and Thoburn's division on the left—the 8th Corps' men readied themselves for the surge toward Lomax's position. For some of the battle-tested troops in Crook's command, success was not a forgone conclusion as they looked at the final preparations being made by the Confederates to meet the assault. "The heaviest abbatis I had ever seen stared us in the face," recalled the 14th West Virginia's Corporal Jesse Tyler Sturm. He continued: "We had the battle of three days before with its terrible death-list fresh in our memory, and it looked like certain death to have to clear away that abbatis under close artillery and musketry fire to scale those works." In his postwar reminiscences, Sturm recalled that he even spied some of the Confederate batteries in support of Lomax's cavalry removing the wheels from the gun carriages "and placing them in their embrasures, digging pits for their gunners, intending thereby to save the recoil of their guns."[153] The 116th Ohio's colonel Thomas Wildes noted simply that the men expected "a fair prospect for some hard fighting, and every man nerved himself for the shock soon to come."[154]

Once Hayes's and Thoburn's divisions steeled their nerves for the attack, Crook gave the order to charge. "With one wild yell, we burst from that mountain-side," recalled a veteran of the Thirty-fourth Massachusetts, "like an avalanche of howling demons, on the rebel left."[155] As Crook's infantry rushed down the mountainside into a ravine, all order among the ranks disappeared, with men running at different rates of speed. By "the time we arrived at the foot of the mountain and emerged from the woods, our lines were completely broken," Crook recalled.[156] A soldier in the Fourteenth West Virginia recorded after the war: "We soon lost all formation, and were in a general mixup with bushes and greenbriars and grapevines."[157] Crook's men knew what needed to be accomplished and did not waste time reforming broken ranks. Each of Crook's men became his own general as they surged toward the Confederate left flank. "Thence we went, sweeping down their works like a western cyclone, every man for himself," remembered Colonel Thomas Wildes, "firing whenever he saw a rebel and always yelling and cheering to the extent of his ability."[158]

"Crook, Hayes, and Thoburn, were nominally commanders," observed a Union officer, "and were here, there, everywhere in the mass, but really were but integral parts, of a legion of shouting fighting demons. No orders were given, as these veterans knew well what to do."[159]

The first substantial force Crook's regiments encountered were troops from Lomax's cavalry division. Colonel Charles T. O'Ferrall, who commanded a contingent of three hundred dismounted troopers at Fisher's Hill as part of Lomax's command, had his men in position behind "rail piles" and "rifle pits."[160] The various defenses constructed by Lomax's men in the days leading up to the battle gave little confidence to Lomax about his commands' ability to successfully stymie the Union onslaught. "Having only a few intrenching [*sic*] tools, borrowing from time to time from the infantry," Lomax explained in his report of the battle written over one month after the engagement, "the line was not made a strong one; it was naturally very weak."[161]

Some of Lomax's men could not believe their eyes and initially looked on in astonishment at the scene of Crook's advance. The Eighteenth Virginia Cavalry's Private Isaac N. Baker, charged with holding a contingent of horses, was startled into the reality of battle when the horse standing right next to him "tore from" him "with such force that the bridle strap tore some flesh from" his hand. Baker and other members of the regiment who held horses immediately released them so that they could fight. Now scores of scrambling horses exacerbated an already bad situation. "I pulled my gun and commenced fighting...The other boys let the horses go and did the same. This stampeded the horses...the fighting...in front...made an awful noise that frightened the horses more than ever," Baker recorded.[162]

What continued to worsen the now deplorable state of affairs for Lomax's command was that, as it readjusted its line to meet Crook's attack coming from the west, troops from Keifer's brigade, artillery from the Sixth Corps and Union troops from Averell's division pressured the portion of Lomax's line that fronted north.[163] Lomax appealed to Ramseur for help to man the thinned defenses, but the support never arrived. "I immediately changed my front to meet his force, notifying the nearest division infantry commander [Ramseur] of the fact, and asking that the works left by me should be immediately occupied...The infantry

General Lunsford Lomax. *Photographic History of the Civil War.*

failed to come to my support," reported the much-maligned Lomax after the battle.[164]

Although Lomax believed that Ramseur had stood idly by while his troopers met the Union onslaught, Ramseur did, in fact, take action. When the flank attack commenced, Ramseur, having received no direction from Early, ordered General William Cox's brigade of North Carolinians to support Lomax. Ramseur offered no specific directive to Cox other than to withdraw his brigade from the main line and "move in the direction of the firing."[165] As Cox marched his command toward the sound of the battle, however, he veered too far to the southwest and completely bypassed Crook's command. Cox eventually did encounter Lomax, but that juncture came well after Lomax's troopers had fled from their position.[166]

Lomax's men, although abused in much of the writings on the battle, did what they could to resist the Union onslaught coming at them from the west and north. Colonel O'Ferrall noted that the Confederate artillery that supported Lomax's troopers "was pouring shell, grape, and canister into the mass that was sweeping down the mountain slope, but to no visible effect." O'Ferrall wrote four decades after the war that as he "saw the mighty horde coming," he withdrew his command "a short distance to higher ground" and then ordered a charge. When a piece of shrapnel struck O'Ferrall's right knee and knocked him to the ground, he reported that his men lost all confidence in an attack and "broke and scattered in every direction." The efforts of Lomax's men—a command outnumbered by a margin of nearly five to one—to slow the Union onslaught proved futile.[167]

As Lomax's command scattered from the battlefield, some of his troopers reportedly encountered infantryman atop Fisher's Hill and spread a panic among them. "While standing in position, a cavalryman from out left came down our line," remembered the Thirteenth Virginia captain, Samuel D. Buck, "reporting to each command that we are flanked…the worthless soldier should have been shot then and there."[168]

From the perspective of the infantry who manned the main Confederate line on Fisher's Hill, Lomax's troopers did not do nearly enough to slow the Union tidal wave. Lomax and his command, however, vociferously attested that they could not have done more under the circumstances. Confederate cavalryman French Harding explained that "General Lomax did his best and tried to stop it with his almost unsupported artillery but failed. Five or six to one was too much odds."[169]

As Lomax's cavalry gave way to the "western cyclone" of Crook's attack, Ramseur readied his division, sans Cox's brigade. Ramseur moved General Cullen Battle's brigade of Alabamians to a position that faced to the west. Battle, who earlier that day had received a communication from Early praising him for his conduct at the Third Battle of Winchester three days earlier, found himself in a most unenviable position as his brigade of

Sketch of Crook's attack against the Confederate left flank defended by Lomax and Ramseur. *Author's collection.*

General Cullen Andrews Battle. *MOLLUS, U.S. Army Military History Institute.*

battle-tested veterans attempted to do what Lomax's command could not: stave off disaster.[170]

While Battle readied his brigade, Kirkpatrick's Amherst Battery, part of Colonel Thomas Nelson's artillery battalion, wheeled its guns by hand and faced them to the west. Troops from Thoburn's division bore the brunt of the fire from Kirkpatrick's cannon. Nelson offered support to Battle's and Kirkpatrick's men by positioning the guns of Massie's Fluvanna Battery behind Battle's brigade. One of Massie's gunners noted that, after being "pulled out of the breastworks" to support Battle, Massie's battery "was pouring canister into the ranks of the advancing Yankees, with as much vim as if we could have hoped to drive them back…It was very much like the combat between David & Goliath."[171]

Steeled by the incessant fire of Kirkpatrick's and Massie's guns, General Battle did what he could to inspire his men. Through the din of the fight, a Confederate artillerist, M.S. Watts, saw Battle, a "distinguished looking officer with buck-skin gauntlets, and gold braid," urging his men to hold their ground at all hazards by brandishing a cedar stake which Battle reportedly pulled from a nearby fence. Battle's voice cut through the air as Watts heard the Alabamian shout, "Close-up! On your life!"[172]

For a moment, Battle's efforts and those of Massie's and Kirkpatrick's cannons slowed Crook's advance. Colonel Thoburn noted that Battle's men made "a more stubborn resistance, and our advance for a short time was driven back."[173] Crook penned of the impact of Battle's defenders: "The batteries from the bluffs…together with some troops…were making the ground hot for us." As the musket and artillery fire slowed the Union attack, Crook's temper flared; some of his men refused to advance any farther. An infuriated Crook grabbed rocks from the ground and pelted these soldiers to urge them back into action. Crook wrote after the war that this effort "made it so uncomfortable for this rear that they tarried no longer."[174]

While Crook's attack might have initially slowed in this battle of "David and Goliath"—one in which the "David" would not win—the gunners in Kirkpatrick's and Massie's commands knew they would not be able to fend off the Union Goliath indefinitely, so as the battle raged, concern among the artillerists grew over how they were going to prevent their guns from falling into Union hands. When Kirkpatrick's gunners wheeled their cannons, to the west, all the battery's horses stood about one mile behind the main Confederate line, grazing. No man could be spared from the front to collect the horses, so the battery's chaplain, Reverend Thomas W. Gilmer, "volunteered to go and bring up the horses."[175]

An artillerist in Kirkpatrick's Battery recalled that Reverend Gilmer brought up the horses "very quickly," and the gunners hitched up the teams to safely withdraw the guns. As Kirkpatrick's fire stopped so that the guns could be removed from the field, the artillerists stood in awe at the mettle of Battle's command, which fought desperately to buy precious moments for the artillery's safe evacuation. One of Kirkpatrick's artillerists noted that in the effort to evacuate the artillery, "Battle's Brigade...behaved splendidly."[176]

Although Battle's brigade "behaved splendidly," Colonel William Nelson, the artillery battalion commander whose guns protected the army's left flank, knew that when Crook's command got closer, he would have no choice but to evacuate all three of his batteries. Nelson ordered his battery commanders to withdraw several guns at a time and then instructed them to, as they pulled back toward the Valley Pike, go a distance, find advantageous ground, unlimber and fire so as to slow the enemy onslaught. Although Nelson's battalion lost four cannons in the fight, one chronicler noted that "Col. Nelson's conduct was conspicuously gallant as he withdrew his pieces in small groups, alternately unlimbering and firing and entirely without infantry support."[177]

One of the guns Nelson was not able to safely extricate from the field was a rifled gun from Kirkpatrick's Battery, which was posted near the apex of the angle where Ramseur's division bent its line back to the west. The gunners, to their credit, did not flinch as troops from Colonel Joseph Thoburn's division—posted on the left of Crook's line—surged toward the Confederate position. Colonel George Wells, who commanded Thoburn's lead brigade, noted that, as his troops spied that cannon, they did not hesitate but rather seemed inspired "with new ardor." The 116th Ohio rushed straight toward the gun "without an

Colonel George Wells. *Author's collection.*

instant's hesitation." At a distance of around one hundred yards, in Colonel Wells's estimation, the Confederate cannon unleashed its charge of canister, but the survivors of the regiment, supported by the 34th Massachusetts captured the gun "in the very smoke of its discharge."[178]

On the other end of Crook's line, the men of Hayes's division surged toward the Confederate cannons from Nelson's battalion. A soldier in the Fourteenth West Virginia, part of Lieutenant Colonel Benjamin Coates's brigade, noted that Nelson's gunners "fought like demons."[179]

As Nelson's battalion withdrew, the weight of Crook's attack became too much for Battle's brigade to endure. The task of fending off the onslaught now rested on the shoulders of General Grimes. By the time Battle's brigade withdrew, the Confederate left confronted pressure not only from the west but also from the north. When Crook had launched his attack, the Union assault plan called for Ricketts's division to support Crook's left and move against Ramseur's division. While Crook urged his corps forward and engaged Lomax's troopers, he saw Ricketts standing still. Crook thought that this might turn into a repeat of the Battle of Cool Spring fought two months earlier, when Ricketts was ordered to support Crook's command but failed to do so. "Gen. Ricketts made a temporary halt," Crook remembered. The general continued: "I feared he was about to leave us to our fate, but he soon moved."[180]

Though Grimes had taken the initiative before the attack commenced to reposition his line, his redeployment did little to stem the tide. As Crook's divisions rushed forward, his line was so long that Hayes's division actually overlapped the Confederate left and fired into the Confederate rear. Grimes's brigade now took fire from three directions. Grimes wrote to his wife: "The enemy attacked me on my left flank, front and rear at the same time." Confronted with this impossible situation, General Ramseur rode onto the scene and ordered Grimes to withdraw his brigade "if possible." At the moment Ramseur gave Grimes that directive, Grimes estimated that the Union forces stood about one hundred yards away from his brigade. "The colors of the United States troops were then in less than a hundred of yards to me," Grimes wrote three days after the battle.[181]

After Grimes ordered his five regiments to withdraw from their unenviable position, he searched desperately for a horse to carry him to safety. Before the battle had begun, Grimes thought that the bulk of the fighting would be done that day in the earthworks constructed by the infantry in the days prior to the battle and so had sent his horse to a hollow in the rear of the Confederate line. Without an opportunity to secure his mount, Grimes searched desperately for another. Fleeing on foot was not an option for Grimes, as earlier in the day, he had fallen and badly sprained his ankle. Grimes noted that he "was able to hobble along, but very slowly." The rush of the Union attack prompted Grimes to conclude that if he did not secure a mount quickly, he "would be left behind to fall into the hands of the Yankees." As he contemplated his fate, a Union artillery shell tore through the air and struck two horses and a caisson, presumably from one of Nelson's retreating cannons. While the artillerists struggled to get the other horses loose from their harnesses, Grimes "vaulted" himself into the saddle of one of the horses still attached to the caisson. He pleaded with an unidentified artillerist to cut his horse loose as well, but as Grimes explained to his wife, the artillerist "didn't take time to parley with me, but ran off leaving the horse still fastened by one trace to the horse that had been killed." Grimes took out his own knife, cut himself free and "put spurs" to his new mount. As he dashed toward the Valley Pike in his "miraculous escape," he found the Forty-fifth North Carolina's Colonel John Winston "broken down." Grimes grabbed Winston and rode southeast. With his safety secured, Grimes now focused his attention on reorganizing his broken brigade and slowing the enemy onslaught.[182]

With three of Ramseur's brigades rushing "pell-mell from their position," the final brigade in Ramseur's division, General Philip Cook's brigade of four Georgia regiments, did little to slow the Union attack. As the division withdrew from the battlefield, Early rode onto the scene to figure out how to stem the tide and save his army. As Early surveyed the field, he ordered the division that protected his eastern flank, General Gabriel Wharton's, to move from its position to check the Union attack.[183] While Early's cartographer Jedediah Hotchkiss and several other staff officers rode off to the east to get Wharton's division, Early knew he needed to buy time for the redeployment.[184]

With Ramseur's regiments streaming to the southeast, he rode up to the left-most regiment of General John Pegram's division, the Thirteenth Virginia Infantry, and ordered it to do the unthinkable—stop the retreating mass of soldiers from Ramseur's division by threatening to shoot them if they refused. The Thirteenth Virginia's captain, Samuel Buck, could not believe Early's directive. "Gen. Early rode up and ordered our regiment to fire into them if they would not halt," Buck remembered. The veterans of the Thirteenth refused to obey the order.[185]

Unable to stop Ramseur's division from retreating and powerless to get Pegram's troops to stop the retreat, Early's position atop the valley's Gibraltar now seemed hopeless against the Union tidal wave sweeping violently from the west. Hopelessness quickly transitioned into despair as Sheridan ordered the remaining troops of the Union Sixth and Nineteenth Corps to press Early's beleaguered army from the north. The deplorable circumstances would soon turn into, as one Confederate termed it, a complete and utter "disgrace."[186]

Chapter Four

"A Confused Delirious Mass"

As Ramseur's brigades succumbed to the pressure from Crook's flank attack and the additional pressure applied from the north by Ricketts's division, one of Ricketts's brigade commanders, Colonel Keifer, wanted to find a way into the interior of the earthworks abandoned by Ramseur's division. As Keifer navigated the terrain in the midst of the battle up the "steep hill," he encountered a "mounted officer wearing a plain blouse and a slouch hat, but with no insignia of rank." Uncertain of the rider's identity, Keifer rode with this "mounted officer "for a short time." Keifer inquired if he "knew what General Crook was then doing." The mysterious officer "modestly laughed, and said Crook was just then engaged with me in gaining an entrance to the enemy's fortifications, and that he supposed his command was pursuing Early." Keifer wrote decades after the war that his introduction "to the hero of this battle" in the midst of the Union assault quickly "ripened into a friendship" that endured until Crook's death in 1890.[187]

With the success of Crook's assault and the additional pressure from Ricketts's division, the task of clearing the rest of Early's army from the heights of Fisher's Hill now fell on the other two divisions of Wright's Sixth Corps and Emory's Nineteenth Corps. For some of the soldiers in Wheaton's and Getty's divisions, "the cheers on the right," signaling Crook's and then Ricketts's success, caused some of the infantryman to get "their blood up," as they knew they would be ordered to assault the heights in front of them and sweep Early's remaining divisions from the battlefield.[188]

Other veterans of Wright's corps seemed a bit anxious about the idea of attacking the Confederate works. At about 4:00 p.m., roughly the same time that Crook launched his assault, the troops from Getty's division moved forward to the crest "immediately in front" of Pegram's division. As Getty's troops moved forward, Confederate artillery, more than likely from Colonel Carter M. Braxton's artillery battalion, unleashed, as General Bidwell recalled, "a heavy artillery fire." Even the corps' commander, General Wright, conceded that initially the ground in front seemed "almost unassailable, the approaches being difficult to climb, and the works covered by abates of no mean strength." Union artillerist Augustus Buell supported Wright's initial observation. "The ground in front of the Rebel works was so steep in many places that it amounted to a natural scarp," Buell explained.[189]

As doubt crept into the minds of some of the Army of the Shenandoah's veterans as to whether or not they could successfully finish the offensive inaugurated by Crook and Ricketts, Sheridan rode onto the scene to inspire his men. A veteran of Wright's command recalled: "Gen. Sheridan rode through the skirmish line on a dead run, sometimes inside and sometimes out…shouting 'Crook and Averell are on their left and rear—we've got 'em,' and it gave us all new courage."[190] Soon after Sheridan's appearance, staff officers, according to an officer in Getty's division, "shouting the glorious news, galloped wildly to the left along the line, sending brigade after brigade to join the charge, and thus the whole army gradually swung into place like machinery."[191]

Wright's brigades, "flushed with the victory of Opequon," surged forward against the Confederate defenses. After navigating the undulating ground in front of Fisher's Hill and various obstacles—such as Tumbling Run—the men of Wright's corps now needed a way to climb the precipitous face of Fisher's Hill, which increased in steepness from west to east. Troops from Wright's corps clawed their way to the top of Early's works to dislodge Pegram's division using whatever means necessary, including pulling themselves up by trees or rocks and even digging bayonets into the ground to negotiate the seemingly impossible terrain.[192]

In addition to the challenges presented by the terrain and Confederate artillery, some of the brigades in the Sixth Corps had to contend with friendly fire. As Bidwell's brigade, on the left of Getty's division, advanced against Pegram's regiments, troops from Colonel James Warner's brigade, who charged in the rear of Bidwell's command, mistakenly fired their muskets into Bidwell's regiments. Bidwell halted his brigade for a moment until the fatal error could be remedied.[193]

With the friendly fire incident between Bidwell's and Warner's brigades resolved, Wright's regiments surged toward the crest of the heights while Crook's and Ricketts's commands still maintained the momentum of the assault from the west. According to most accounts, Pegram's infantry did little to defend its position. Major James H. Coleman of the 102nd Pennsylvania, a regiment in Getty's division, noted that most of Pegram's troops "broke and ran in great confusion" when the surging Union line came to within thirty yards of the Confederate works. Getty recalled in his report of the battle that the "enemy poured in one tremendous volley" as the Union infantry negotiated the terrain and "then broke and fled in the wildest disorder."[194] Alanson A. Haines, the chaplain of the 15th New Jersey, a regiment in Wheaton's division, remembered: "As we sprang toward the rebel works before us, the enemy ran."[195]

General John Pegram. *Library of Congress.*

While Pegram's infantry shattered before the Sixth Corps, the gunners from Braxton's artillery battalion did all that could have been asked of them to slow the Union onslaught. For example, the men of Carpenter's battery stood by their guns until the last moment, "being almost surrounded and about to be pounced upon." As troops from Getty's division swarmed around the guns, Carpenter's artillerymen ceased firing and fled knowing they could not safely withdraw the battery and save themselves. "We had to save ourselves...our guns, caissons, horses, and everything else being captured," bemoaned one of the battery's survivors.[196]

Sketch of the view of the Battle of Fisher's Hill from the northern outskirts of Strasburg with Banks's Fort located on the right side of the image. *Author's collection.*

At least one of Carpenter's guns was seized by troops from the Forty-third New York Battalion. Not complacent to merely have captured the gun, the men of Major Charles A. Milliken's command wanted to use it against the

enemy who had just abandoned it. According to Milliken, three members of the battalion—John Singleton, C. Fitzgerald and Dennis Ganey—"turned and fired one of the guns upon the flying enemy, who were retreating."[197] Once the troops from Getty's and Wheaton's divisions drove Pegram's infantry and Braxton's artillery from their works, the Union battle line, which one veteran of the Union Sixth Corps described as "a confused delirious mass," wheeled to the east to pressure the remaining divisions of Gordon and Wharton.[198]

With so many Confederate artillery pieces falling into Union hands in rapid succession, some of the division and brigade commanders had differences of opinions about how to best secure the artillery while maintaining the consistent pressure of the attack. Some officers, such as Major Milliken, whose New Yorkers turned at least one captured gun on the Confederates, did not believe it prudent to detail men to stay behind and guard the captured artillery: "Thinking that quite a number of prisoners could be captured if the enemy were pursued, I ordered forward the Forty-third, without detailing men to guard the captured guns."[199]

As Milliken's battalion, along with the rest of Bidwell's brigade, continued to press Early's battered command, some of the troops from Bidwell's regiments noted, once again, fire coming from their rear. For the second time in the battle, troops from Colonel Warner's brigade, about five hundred yards behind Bidwell's units, fired inadvertently into the backs of their fellow comrades. Captain David Taylor of the Sixty-first Pennsylvania, a regiment in Bidwell's brigade, recalled of this second friendly fire incident between Warner's and Bidwell's commands: "While still continuing our pursuit of the flying enemy, the First Brigade of our division [Warner's] came up in our rear and near the battery and opened fire with musketry, many of the bullets falling in our ranks, which were nearly 500 yards in advance." Taylor "hurried back and endeavored to stop the firing." While Taylor's efforts eliminated the threat of friendly fire, he could not believe that Colonel Warner "had placed a guard on the guns that we captured."[200]

General Daniel Bidwell. *Library of Congress.*

General Crook, like the troops from Bidwell's brigade, viewed the maintenance of momentum more significant than leaving men behind to guard abandoned Confederate artillery. As the Union assault swept forward, Crook noticed about fifty Union soldiers pulling captured Confederate cannons from the breastworks. Crook surmised that these were his men and vowed to give them a sound verbal thrashing. When he lambasted them for not being at the front, the soldiers informed him that they were not part of Crook's command but instead performed this duty by order of General Ricketts. While Crook sorted out the matter, General Ricketts rode up to the group of infantrymen that he had ordered to pull the guns off the field. When Ricketts saw Crook, the commander of the Eighth Corps recalled that Ricketts "looked as though he was stealing sheep." When Crook informed Ricketts that the paramount objective had to first be the total annihilation of the Confederate line, Ricketts disagreed and believed the security of the captured artillery equally significant. "He wanted to turn them in as his captures," Crook noted of his conversation with Ricketts. Crook tersely informed Ricketts that the men of the Eighth Corps "had been over there sometime previous, and that all able-bodied men were needed at the front."[201]

Although in hindsight the Union attack did not appear to lose any significant momentum while the likes of Ricketts and Warner committed portions of their commands to secure Confederate artillery captured by other units, pockets of Confederate infantry resistance caused brief consternation among some Union officers and made some of them believe not a single man could be spared to secure the trophies of war. For example, following the rout of Pegram's division, a contingent of the 13th Virginia Infantry led by Captain William Aylett Ashby—a native of Culpeper County, Virginia, and a cousin of the famed Confederate general Turner Ashby—took cover in an unidentifiable structure behind Confederate lines and delivered well-aimed shots at Sheridan's infantry as the assault swept forward. Annoyed by this contingent of Confederate marksmen, Lieutenant Robert W. Wiley of the 110th Ohio—along with two privates from the regiment, William Wise and Elias A. Barr, and another private from the 126th Ohio, O.A. Ashbrook—charged Ashby's position and captured the Confederate captain and his contingent of twenty-one men. In the estimation of the 110th Ohio's Lieutenant Colonel Otho Binkley, Wiley and his contingent performed a deed "of valor seldom excelled."[202]

In addition to the futile efforts of Ashby's marksmen, troops from Colonel William R. Peck's Louisiana Brigade, who stood on the left end of Gordon's division near the Manassas Gap Railroad, determined to make

Modern-day view of the area looking southwest from the vicinity of Manassas Gap Railroad trestle toward the position defended by Confederate troops from Colonel William Peck's Louisiana brigade. *Photograph by author.*

a stand, if only to buy a few crucial moments to allow other regiments to escape the battlefield. When Peck's command was "nearly surrounded," the orders finally came to withdraw.[203] After Peck's regiment's received the order, the Louisiana troops "stood not on the order of our going," remembered one veteran of the brigade. Peck's men took to their heels as fast as they could with no care for brigade organization, as had been the case with most of the Confederate units who had withdrawn previously. "It was altogether too late to retire in order," observed an officer in Peck's command, "for it required the greatest fleetness of foot to enable us to keep from being captured."[204]

When Peck's regiments finally executed the order to withdraw, some of his infantryman could not fathom it and begged their comrades to stay and fight, despite the overwhelming odds. A Confederate artillerist recalled being very "much affected" by seeing one Louisiana soldier "behind his comrades crying like a child, and with the tears running down his face." Screaming at the top of his lungs, this Louisiana soldier implored his comrades to stay and fight: "I say men, for God's sake let us stop and fight them right here!" His words fell on deaf ears. The demoralized man from the Louisiana brigade could only muster enough strength to follow his failed plea with a statement that later proved prophetic for Confederate forces in the Shenandoah Valley: "We are ruined forever!"[205]

Although unable to turn the tide of battle or remain and fight for any significant length of time, the fact that Peck's troops did not vacate their line until the last possible moment inspired General Early. With troops streaming to the rear, Early supposedly pointed to Peck's brigade as they confronted initial pressure from Colonel Joseph E. Hamblin's brigade and offered their unwillingness to flee until surrounded "as an example for others to take pattern by." After the battle, Early informed the Louisiana veterans: "If all had stood as you did, the issue would have been different than from what it was."[206]

While Early searched for ways to inspire his men and reorganize his demoralized army, General Sheridan maintained a constant presence on the battlefield and urged his men to be relentless in their pursuit. After the troops from the Union Sixth Corps cleared the Confederate earthworks, wheeled eastward and "advanced rapidly, crossing diagonally over the fields," Sheridan rode behind the men and shouted: "Forward! Forward all! Right ahead, men! Go on, everybody!" Sheridan's encouraging

General Philip Sheridan rallying the men of the Army of the Shenandoah near the close of the battle. *Author's collection.*

words infused additional energy into the Union assault. A veteran of the Fifteenth New Jersey noted that Sheridan's presence "filled" the men "with wild excitement."[207]

As Sheridan rode among his troops, Captain Robert F. Wilkinson, one of Emory's staff officers, dashed along the line of the Nineteenth Corps, vigorously waving his hat in his hand exclaiming: "They've left their guns and are running like cowards!"[208] Although Wilkinson was right, the men of Emory's command had cause to doubt him as the Confederate defenders to their front—Gordon's division supported by artillery from Braxton's battalion—played target practice with them. As the Nineteenth Corps prepared to put the finishing touches on a well-executed attack plan at Fisher's Hill, the Confederate artillery ensconced atop the heights stirred great angst among some of these battle-tested soldiers. A veteran in General Cuvier Grover's division freely admitted: "We were afraid of the shells…those belching cannon, gaping with the leer of demons down upon us…Up there on those cruel heights we saw the Rebel gunners at the liveliest sort of work. They were getting the range with fearful accuracy."[209] Another veteran of the Nineteenth Corps remarked that, as they prepared to advance against Gordon's position, the heights were "bristling with blazing guns."[210] Despite the initial hesitation to attack the eastern end of Fisher's Hill, its most precipitous part, the men did so because they believed in their commanders. A Union chaplain in Colonel Edward Molineux's brigade observed that Emory's men seemed "inspired by the presence of Sheridan."[211] A veteran of the Twenty-ninth Maine echoed: "We marched…resting alone in an abiding faith in Sheridan, believed that he had ordered us to go forward, and knowing, too, that Gen. Emory would not ask of us more than we could do."[212]

While Sheridan's presence might have brought energy to some of Emory's men, at least one member of Emory's corps could have done without it on the battlefield that day—Colonel Molineux. As the Nineteenth Corps advanced, the ground proved impossible for many of Emory's regiments, particularly under the rain of Confederate artillery. The ground in front of Gordon's position traversed, as Molineux recalled, "by an impossible ravine" prompted General Grover to halt the advance momentarily "while he examined the ground." Unaware of Grover's intention, Sheridan fumed with indignation at the halt. Sheridan, Molineux explained in a letter to his sister Nan, "rode up in great excitement and ordered us forward implying we were afraid." Dismayed at having his men labeled as cowards, Molineux went up to Sheridan and told him that the men of Grover's division were "not cowards but are halted by orders." According to Molineux, Sheridan did not want to hear any of it. Understandably frustrated by Sheridan's reaction during the battle, Molineux

Modern-day view of the remnant of the original Valley Pike looking south toward Fisher's Hill. Troops from Colonel Edward Molineux's command passed through this area during their advance. *Photograph by author.*

went so far as to erroneously suggest that alcohol fueled Sheridan's indignation. Molineux wrote: "He dashed up to me excited and under the influence of liquor and cursed me in the most shameful manner before my men."[213]

Sheridan's behavior bothered Molineux to such an extent that, the day after the battle, he went to General Emory and said he wished to resign his commission so that he could "fight Sheridan [in] a duel for insulting" him. Emory intervened on Molineux's behalf and informed Sheridan: "You have insulted one of the best men in my corps. If I had told him to go to hell, he'd have gone." Moved by Emory's comments, Sheridan offered Molineux a public apology. Molineux remembered of Sheridan's apology: "'I had no intention of insulting you. I apologize.' Then he called the company on guard and his staff officers around him and told me he wished to apologize to me for what he had said." In Molineux's estimation, Sheridan's public apology was "the bravest thing Sheridan ever did."[214]

In retrospect, the momentary halt of Grover's division against the eastern flank of Early's line mattered little. By the time Emory's troops reached the

Modern-day view of the remnant of the stone bridge that carried the Valley Pike over Tumbling Run. *Photograph by author.*

base of Fisher's Hill and the stone bridge that carried the Valley Pike across Tumbling Run, Gordon's troops and the Confederate artillery had ceased firing and taken to their heels in retreat, as troops from Crook's corps had swept in behind Gordon's position. As infantry from Emory's corps peered to the top of Fisher's Hill, "those unattainable heights," they spied a color-bearer from one of Crook's regiments. A veteran of the Fourteenth New Hampshire, one of Grover's regiments, recalled that one of Crook's veterans was "waving that resplendent banner with thirty-four stars upon it, signaling to a triumphant army, that, while it was marching up to death in front, victory had been won in the rear."[215]

Now Wharton's command remained the only unbroken one of Early's divisions. As the rout commenced from west to east, Jedediah Hotchkiss attempted to lead Wharton's division, but Wharton had not been able to do much maneuvering to stem Sheridan's onslaught. "Our men came back in a perfect rout," Hotchkiss recalled, "and so rapidly that the enemy was crossing the railroad before the head of the column got into the pike even."[216] With the weight of the Union assault and a panic-stricken mob of Confederate soldiers fleeing for the Valley Pike, the only thing Wharton's division could do at that point was join the retreat.

As Early's army fled the battlefield "in considerable confusion," Sheridan's command tried to maintain some semblance of order as it swept over the Confederate position like "a hurricane."[217] Officers did all they could to keep their regiments organized, but Sheridan cared little about their efforts, as he preferred that his army maintain the momentum of the assault rather than regimental organization. The chaplain of the Fifteenth New Jersey described the scene: "As soon as we had crossed the works, we wheeled to the left, and advanced rapidly, crossing diagonally over the fields to reach the pike. The ground was covered with men, flying and pursuing. Sheridan's only orders were: 'Forward! Forward all! Right ahead men! Go on, everybody!' Our men were filled with wild excitement…We…were all mixed together."[218]

Despite the lack of unit cohesion, the Army of the Shenandoah did not lose a step, and Early's men searched for every possible escape route. While most of Early's command took to the Valley Pike, hundreds of Confederate soldiers fled to the slopes of Massanutten Mountain to avoid falling into Union hands. A veteran from the 116th New York observed that portions of Early's "demoralized…army" ran "by hundreds into the mountain for safety."[219]

Regardless of the best efforts to avoid capture, hundreds of troops from Early's army were taken. The chronicler of the 116th Ohio noted that among the Confederate soldiers captured by his regiment was an unidentified Virginia officer who had a son serving as a private in the 13th West Virginia. Fortuitously, as Union soldiers escorted the unidentified Confederate to the rear, father and son met. "They shook hands," recalled the 116th's regimental historian, "embraced and parted, the father to go to a Northern military prison, the son to continue in the contest."[220]

Some of the Confederates captured by Union troops, at least from the perspective of Sheridan's men, seemed somewhat relieved that they had fallen into Union hands, as now they might have the opportunity to do something that they had not been able to as a part of Early's Valley Army: eat. "No regrets were expressed that the fortunes of war had made them our prisoners. On the contrary," recalled a veteran of Emory's corps, "they manifested real joy at falling into our hands, knowing that they were sure of good rations."[221]

Other Confederates fretted at the prospect of being captured and spending the rest of the conflict as prisoners of war. During the retreat, the Twenty-sixth Georgia's Colonel E.M. Atkinson implored retreating Confederates to assist him in bringing a Confederate artillery piece safely off the battlefield. Atkinson's pleas fell on deaf ears until the Thirty-first

Georgia's I.G. Bradwell offered to help. However, when Sheridan's troops neared the cannon, Bradwell feared capture and abandoned Atkinson. While Bradwell averted capture, Atkinson did not fare so well and was seized by Sheridan's men.[222]

With Early's army routed from its position by the time the sun began to set, some of the soldiers in Sheridan's command hoped that the coming nightfall would give them a chance to rest and eat. "We halted on the heights, expecting to bivouac as darkness had set in, and we were worn out and hungry, not having food since morning," bemoaned a veteran of the 128th New York.[223] A veteran of the 116th New York echoed: "To say that we were tired would not in any measure express our condition. We were exhausted with the hard and constant duties of the preceding four days. Daylight was fast fading away, and at every step we expected an order to halt and make ourselves comfortable for the night."[224]

Sheridan, however, had no intention of halting his pursuit for any great length of time. Once the entire Army of the Shenandoah concentrated near the Valley Pike, Sheridan's subordinates spent about one hour reorganizing their commands and preparing to resume the chase.[225] During that period of reorganization, pure jubilation overtook Sheridan's army, as the men rent the air with shouts of exultation at driving Early's army from its seemingly impenetrable position. "Never was an army happier," recalled the Fourteenth New Hampshire's Francis Buffum. He continued: "Every regiment cheered every other regiment that it passed. They roared and bellowed and whooped; and every man of us was away inside the truth when he declared, that he 'never yelled so in all his life.'"[226] After looking at the condition of his men, Sheridan determined to halt the Eighth Corps. Sheridan recognized that of all the troops in his army, Crook's regiments had done the most and deserved a much-needed rest. The army commander directed Crook's "tired, exhausted men…to give up the pursuit and go into camp."[227]

While Crook's command rested and Wright's Sixth Corps reorganized ranks, Sheridan turned to the one infantry corps that experienced the least amount of action on the twenty-second: Emory's. Sheridan now looked to Emory's command to assume the burden of pursuing Early's tattered army through the night. Among those who did not approve of the night pursuit was Colonel Molineux. With his public chastisement still fresh in his mind, Molineux thought that Sheridan's desire to pursue Early through the night "was a most horrid thing and unmilitary." Molineux again erroneously charged that Sheridan made that order because the army commander "was at that time furiously drunk."[228]

Despite Molineux's misgivings, he obeyed Sheridan's directive and led the van of Emory's pursuit. Molineux, who feared "any dash of cavalry which might annoy the head of the column," ordered one company of the Fourteenth New Hampshire to fix bayonets and move "some distance in advance" of the brigade to block any attempt by Early's cavalry to slow the pursuit.[229] Although angst gripped Molineux as his command advanced on the Valley Pike, the troops he commanded seemed not only jubilant but also somewhat complacent. A veteran of the Fourteenth New Hampshire noted that the troops of Molineux's lead regiment "led the pursuing column at a good smart pace, singing, whistling, and bantering jokes at the expense of the flying Johnnies." The sense of "hilarity" and "merriment" quickly dissipated by the time the head of Molineux's column reached Mount Prospect, several miles south of Fisher's Hill.[230]

During the Confederate retreat from Fisher's Hill, Jedediah Hotchkiss determined to do something to organize an impediment to any further Union pursuit. As Hotchkiss tried to "stop the mass of fugitives on the top of the hill near Mount Prospect," four Confederate officers—General Gordon, General Pegram, Early's chief of staff Lieutenant Colonel Alexander "Sandie" Pendleton and the Thirteenth Virginia's Captain Buck—joined him in his attempt to do the impossible.[231] This cadre of Confederate officers rallied a variety of units, including troops from Battle's brigade, Cox's brigade and the Thirteenth Virginia. Two artillery pieces under the watchful gaze of Captain Joseph Carpenter supported this effort.[232]

While this makeshift Confederate force did its best to establish a defensive position at Mount Prospect, a contingent of Confederates advanced north, ground over which Early's army had retreated, in order to erect various obstacles to slow any pursuit, including stringing wire across the Valley Pike. Four days after the battle, Colonel Molineux described the efforts of this small group of Confederates: "Wire and other obstacles had been placed to delay the skirmish line."[233]

As the head of Molineux's column neared Mount Prospect, the two Confederate cannons, which in Molineux's estimation "were well trained upon the road," unleashed canister. One Confederate artillerist recalled decades after the conflict of the two Confederate artillery pieces at Mount Prospect: "Never were the iron messengers of death hurled in quicker succession from the throats of two guns."[234]

The artillery fire, soon followed by the rattle of Confederate muskets, stymied Molineux's lead regiment, the Fourteenth New Hampshire. A veteran of the regiment recorded of the opening salvos near Mount Prospect: "Suddenly a streak of fire a quarter of a mile long flashed along the opposite hillside, and the rattle of musketry followed. The bullets flew thick about us…All was confusion…It was pitch dark, and no one could determine the strength of the demonstration."[235] As the veterans of the Fourteenth New Hampshire recoiled from the shock, the confusing mêlée was exacerbated by a problem that had manifested itself several times during the fight at Fisher's Hill: friendly fire.

Molineux's lead regiment soon realized that the biggest threat rested not with the Confederates in its front but with its comrades behind them, who became unnerved by the Confederate muzzle flashes. "We were in more danger from Union muskets in the rear than from the enemy," recalled a veteran of the Fourteenth New Hampshire. Caught in a maelstrom of bullets fired from two different directions, some of Molineux's veterans attempted to retreat south. An officer in Emory's corps noted that "a panic seemed imminent."[236] Undoubtedly enraged by the friendly fire, Colonel Molineux sent word to the regiments behind the Fourteenth New Hampshire to stop firing.[237] Under the steady leadership of Captain Theodore F. Ripley, the New Hampshire men formed a line of battle on the west side of the Valley Pike and were soon joined by other elements of Molineux's brigade.[238]

While Molineux's men regained their composure, Sandie Pendleton, astride a white horse, did all he could to steel the nerves of the Confederate defenders who "were firing rapidly" with the "bullets…coming thick and fast." No sooner had Henry Kyd Douglas, a member of Early's staff and one of Pendleton's closest friends, urged Pendleton to get off the horse than the Thirteenth Virginia's Captain Buck heard "the familiar 'thud' and knew a bullet had struck either Pendleton or his horse." It was Pendleton and not his horse who had fallen victim to a Union bullet. Shot in the groin and through the body, Douglas noted that his dear friend "gave a groan and tottered forward on his horse."[239]

Pendleton fell "gently" off his mount into Douglas's arms. Although severely wounded, Pendleton tried desperately to stand, to no avail. As the fire from Emory's corps "became more galling," the Confederate line at Mount Prospect began to give way. Fearing for Pendleton's safety, Douglas, along with "several strong men," carried Pendleton to the rear and placed him in an ambulance. By the time he was placed in the ambulance, Pendleton knew he was mortally wounded and had perhaps only a few hours to live. Pendleton handed over his personal effects to Douglas, who wrote of the powerful moment: "He told me he was mortally wounded. He gave me his watch, pocketbooks, prayer book, Bible, and haversack." In addition to asking Douglas to care for his personal items, Pendleton implored Douglas to write to Pendleton's pregnant wife, Kate—a woman to whom Pendleton had been married for slightly less than nine months—"of his death."[240]

By the time Pendleton had been shot, the brief Confederate resistance at Mount Prospect had disintegrated, and a chaotic scene again ensued with "wagons, caissons, limbers, artillery, and flying men" streaming "down the pike toward Woodstock."[241] Among the rolling stock moving hastily south was the ambulance that carried General Early's mortally wounded chief of staff. The ambulance took Pendleton to the home of Dr. Murphy in Woodstock. The Murphy residence, known to many in the Confederate army as "that home of beauty, graciousness, and boundless hospitality…that home of all Confederates in need," now served the role of hospital for Pendleton.[242]

Lieutenant Colonel Alexander "Sandie" Pendleton, mortally wounded near Mount Prospect. *Preston Library, Virginia Military Institute Archives.*

When Pendleton arrived at Murphy's home, Dr. Hunter McGuire tended to his wounds and confirmed that they were mortal. Resigned to his fate, Pendleton stated, "It is God's will, I am satisfied."[243] McGuire did what he could to ease Pendleton's suffering so that, in the young staff officer's final hours "between the paroxysms of pain," he could send "messages of love to his wife and other relatives and friends."[244]

Around midnight, Dr. McGuire learned that the Confederate rear guard, which occupied Woodstock to cover the retreat of what remained of Early's army, was making preparations to march south toward Mount Jackson with the rest of Early's command. McGuire informed Pendleton that he would "remain with him to the last at the risk of being made prisoner."[245] Pendleton would not allow it and instead encouraged McGuire to join Early's main force and "fall back with the army, where he could be of so much service."[246] McGuire agreed and left Woodstock shortly after midnight.[247]

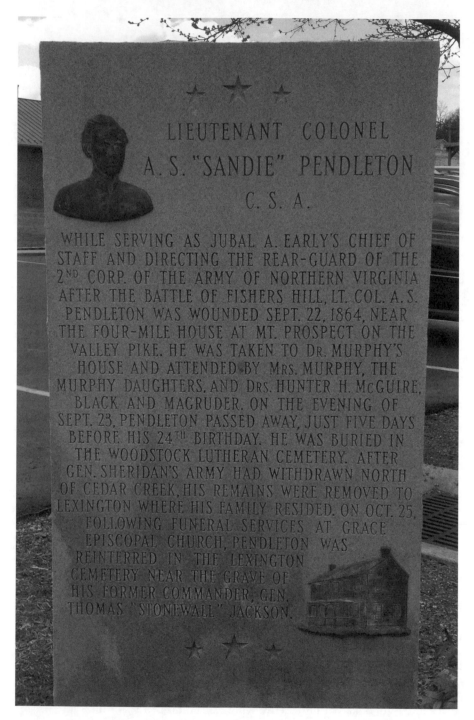

Monument in Woodstock, Virginia, marking the home of Dr. Murphy, where Pendleton died. *Photograph by author.*

In the hours after McGuire's departure, Pendleton's condition worsened rapidly to the point that those who tended him, including Union doctors who "proffered any aid in their power," noted that he became delirious and incessantly craved ice.[248] During the evening of September 23, Pendleton, five days shy of his twenty-fourth birthday and leaving behind a pregnant wife, died. Pendleton's body was buried in the Lutheran Cemetery in Woodstock. The town's Confederate civilians "kept" Pendleton's grave "covered with flowers" until the latter part of October, when his remains were moved to his hometown of Lexington for permanent interment. Pendleton was laid to rest on October 25, 1864, in what is today known as the Stonewall Jackson Memorial Cemetery.[249]

News of Pendleton's death devastated those who knew and admired him. Mary Greenhow Lee, one of Winchester's staunchest Confederate civilians, could not believe the news of Pendleton's passing. Lee confided in her journal two days after Pendleton's death: "I am so grieved to hear of Sandy [sic] Pendleton's death."[250] General Early remarked that Pendleton was "a gallant and efficient young officer…He was acting with his accustomed gallantry, and his loss was deeply felt and regretted."[251] To some Confederate officers, such as Colonel William Allan, Pendleton's loss was not merely about losing a quality soldier but represented the futility of the conflict as it abruptly ended the life of someone who held such great potential for future success. Reflecting on Pendleton's life seven years after his death in a memorial volume for Confederate soldiers killed in the Civil War who had attended the University of Virginia, Allan penned: "In the long catalogue of youthful sons who sprang to arms at her bidding and fell in her defence, Virginia mourns no one more worthy of her grand renown, or whose opening life gave promise of a more useful and distinguished future."[252]

While Pendleton clung desperately to life at Dr. Murphy's, Sheridan's troops moved methodically toward Woodstock. Several miles south of Mount Prospect, near Tom's Brook, Emory's troops again ran into some Confederates who attempted to slow the Union pursuit. For a moment, the fire stymied the Union advance, but the Nineteenth Corps' veterans regained their composure and continued to press forward. After the brief encounter near Tom's Brook, one of Emory's division commanders, General Dwight, in an effort to protect his men, informed his troops to "keep quiet and not be so anxious to rush ahead." When Dwight offered his cautionary note, Sheridan stood within earshot and could not believe the words that came from Dwight's mouth. Sheridan desired the army to move as rapidly as possible. He went up to Dwight and, in the estimation of an officer in the Nineteenth

Corps, gave the division commander "the most unreasonable and profane rebuke that we ever heard from our distinguished commander."[253]

As Sheridan's hungry and fatigued army moved closer to Woodstock, it received a boost to its spirit when it learned from area civilians that Early's army was "ahead running like hounds." This information, noted an officer in Emory's command, "was almost as good as a supper!"[254] Finally, about 4:00 a.m. on September 23, the Army of the Shenandoah occupied Woodstock. Unfortunately, the Confederates were long gone by that point. As much as Sheridan might have wanted to maintain his pursuit of Early's command, the Army of the Shenandoah suffered from exhaustion and desperately needed rest and a meal.[255] A veteran of Emory's corps noted that once the men stacked their muskets in "a field beyond the town," the "men were so weary that most of them slept until ten o'clock, like logs."[256]

While Sheridan's troops rested on a rainy September 23 and waited for rations, Sheridan took the opportunity to write to General Grant a brief note informing him of the army's success at Fisher's Hill.[257] "The rebels threw down their arms and fled in the greatest confusion," Sheridan informed his superior in part, "abandoning most of their artillery...I pursued on after the enemy during the night to this point [Woodstock], with the Sixth and Nineteenth Army Corps, and have stopped here to rest the men and issue rations...The number of pieces of artillery reported captured is sixteen." Although casualty figures for the battle had not yet been reported, Sheridan informed Grant that "our loss will be light." Sheridan's estimation proved correct. Although the casualty numbers for the Army of the Shenandoah differ slightly based on accounts and usually range between 450 and approximately 500 casualties, official reports place Sheridan's total loss in killed, wounded and captured at Fisher's Hill at 456.[258]

General Early, on the other hand, suffered more than double the casualties of Sheridan's command. Several weeks after the battle, Early reported to General Lee that he suffered a total of 1,235 casualties at Fisher's Hill, including nearly 1,000 missing.[259]

As the armies moved south, civilians in the vicinity of Fisher's Hill came out of hiding to aid army doctors in caring for the wounded. The Barbe family home, which had served as General Lomax's headquarters prior to the battle, now played the role of hospital. One account states that, at one point in the aftermath of the battle, at least thirty wounded soldiers lay shoulder to shoulder on the house's side porch waiting for medical attention.[260] In the 1890s, Emma Howard Wright interviewed someone whom she ambiguously identified as "an old farmer" who lived in an "old farm-house at the foot of the North Mountain" during the battle. Although this man's identity might never be fully known to the satisfaction of scholars, Wright recounted that this farmer and his family spent the weeks following the engagement tending to dozens of wounded Union soldiers, and his farm was transformed into an ersatz hospital. During the interview, the farmer informed Wright: "After the battle of Fisher's Hill, the surgeons were very busy here among the wounded…Some had gone mad with agony, and I saw one poor fellow jerk off his arm, as it hung by a few pieces of flesh, stare at it for a moment, with a hideous grin on his ghastly face, and then fall back dead."[261] Several miles to the east, Rebecca Funkhouser, whose family farm stood on the east side of the Valley Pike and slightly south of Early's main line, did what she could to aid wounded Union soldiers. Her efforts in caring for around fifty of Sheridan's wounded men might have actually saved the family's farm. During Sheridan's scorched earth campaign after Fisher's Hill, he ordered his troops to burn the Funkhouser barn. She confronted Sheridan's men and

The Funkhouser home and its outbuildings became the site of one of the many ersatz hospitals in the aftermath of the fight. The care given by Miss Rebecca Funkhouser to around fifty wounded Union soldiers after the battle saved the property from destruction during "the Burning." *David J. Garms collection.*

told them that at the time she still cared for scores of wounded Union troops. When Sheridan heard this, he ordered "his men to pass on."[262]

While the Army of the Shenandoah pushed south, Sheridan undoubtedly reveled at the light loss of men and the completeness of the rout of Early's army, but he still did not feel that he could give Grant "any definite account of the results of the battle" because Sheridan had not yet received any word from his cavalry commander General Torbert, who had been sent on a mission to the Luray Valley to cut off Early's retreat route. Sheridan knew that if "Torbert had pushed down the Luray Valley according to my directions, he will achieve great results."[263]

Sheridan had high hopes for his cavalry. At the Third Battle of Winchester, they had delivered the final crushing blow to Early's army, and now, after the rout of Confederate forces at Fisher's Hill, Sheridan hoped they could do the same by cutting off Early's army before it reached New Market. Unfortunately, the Union cavalry dashed Sheridan's hopes of achieving "results still more pregnant" from the great success on September 22.[264]

Chapter Five

"Another Glorious Union Victory Has Been Gained"

S heridan anxiously awaited news from Torbert on September 23. Sheridan firmly believed that the troopers from General James H. Wilson's division and two brigades from General Wesley Merritt's division—around 5,000 Union cavalry—under Torbert's leadership would be able to easily push aside the nearly 1,500 Confederate horsemen commanded by General Williams C. Wickham in the Luray Valley. Once Torbert crushed Wickham, Sheridan hoped Torbert's cavalry could then race to New Market and cut off Early's retreat route. If achieved, Sheridan concluded that he had "no doubt" that "the entire rebel army" would be captured.[265]

Torbert's operation in the Luray Valley began with success at Front Royal on September 21. As Torbert's cavalry passed south through Front Royal toward Luray, the town's civilians feared the Union cavalry would sever Early's retreat route should he have to withdraw from Fisher's Hill. Lucy Buck confided in her diary on the evening of September 21, after Torbert's cavalry brigades passed through Front Royal: "Everyone uneasy about Early, for this evening two divisions of cavalry passed through town en route for Luray, and if they cannot in some way be checked, they will flank him."[266]

Buck's hope that Torbert's detachment could be "checked" came to fruition the day after Wickham's troopers withdrew from Front Royal. At Milford, a small hamlet about twelve miles south of Front Royal located along the South Fork of the Shenandoah River, Colonel Thomas T. Munford, who assumed command of the cavalry contingent while Wickham sought out General Early, arrayed his cavalry in a strong position to block Torbert's advance.

Munford placed his men on high ground with Overall's Run between him and his Union counterparts. The Confederate left flank rested on the South Fork of the Shenandoah River while Munford's right flank anchored on the Blue Ridge Mountains. Confederate cavalry strengthened the position by constructing "loop-hole breast-works, which extended clear across the valley."[267]

Torbert arrived in front of Munford's ensconced position about 11:00 a.m. on the twenty-second and determined that, instead of launching a direct assault, he would soften Munford's position with artillery. Munford recalled that Torbert's artillery "commenced a furious shelling," to which the cannons of Major James Breathed's "battery answered with a vigor."[268] While the artillery dueled and elements of Torbert's cavalry exchanged fire with troops from the Virginians of Colonel William Payne's brigade, Munford received word from one of his scouts that he thought Torbert might be attempting to move a "considerable force" to take the

Top: General Alfred T.A. Torbert. *Library of Congress.*

Bottom: Colonel Thomas Munford. *Photographic History of the Civil War.*

Modern-day view from Munford's line of defense looking north toward Front Royal. *Photograph by author.*

Confederate position by flanking the eastern end of Munford's line anchored on the Blue Ridge. In an effort to deter any attack, Munford decided to employ a bit of psychological warfare against his Union counterparts.

Munford ordered the Fourth Virginia to withdraw from its main line and move into position to block any attempt by Torbert's cavalry to either turn the eastern flank or get into Munford's rear. When the Fourth Virginia moved out to redeploy on foot, Munford ordered the buglers from the First, Second and Fourth Virginia to space themselves out "about regimental distance apart." Munford informed these three buglers that whenever his "headquarters' bugle sounded the advance, they were to echo the same notes, one following the other." The Confederate cavalry commander hoped that the ruse might cause Torbert to think Munford moved a brigade of cavalry rather than one regiment. The tactic of deception worked. "I had the bugle for the advance sounded," Munford explained, "and it was responded to in turn by the other three. The echo up the crags and cliffs pealed and reverberated...back they [Torbert's men] went in a hurry."[269]

The buglers' ruse, coupled with the stout defense of Munford's command and the nature of the terrain, convinced Torbert that he could not dare attack the position, despite the numerical superiority of his command. "The length of their line was very short," Torbert noted of the Confederate position and his decision to withdraw, "and the banks of the creek so precipitous, it was impossible for the men to get across in order to make a direct attack." Unaware of events west of Massanutten Mountain, Torbert deemed it more prudent to keep his command intact rather than risk a disastrous assault against unfavorable terrain. Torbert explained his decision to not engage Munford and retrace his steps north toward Front Royal: "Not knowing that the army had made an attack at Fisher's Hill, and thinking that the sacrifice would be too great to attack without that knowledge, I concluded to withdraw."[270]

Sheridan received word of Torbert's decision at some point before noon on September 23.[271] Little Phil could not believe that Torbert made no "serious effort at all to dislodge the Confederate cavalry." While Sheridan conceded that the Confederate position at Milford "was a strong one," he still believed "Torbert ought to have made a fight." Sheridan recalled more than two decades after the battle that Torbert's "impotent attempt not only chagrined me very much, but occasioned much unfavorable comment throughout the army."[272]

Already incensed over Torbert's lack of aggressiveness in the Luray Valley, Sheridan fumed with indignation at the inability of General Averell's division of cavalry to join Colonel Thomas Devin's cavalry brigade (part of Merritt's division) and pursue Early aggressively. When Averell finally reached Woodstock around noon on the twenty-third, the division commander explained to Sheridan that his men had great difficulty navigating the terrain on the Back Road. "The road was so hilly and indirect that I was delayed," Averell explained. Furthermore, Averell contended that Sheridan provided "no information or instructions" as to what needed to be done once the three infantry corps cleared Early's command from Fisher's Hill. Sheridan told Averell that he tried to find the division commander but could not. Angry over the insinuation that he had somehow shirked his responsibilities, Averell inquired if Sheridan "had tried."[273] Sheridan cared little for Averell's explanation and tone. After the two generals exchanged "some hot words," Sheridan provided Averell an opportunity to redeem himself.[274]

Still believing Early's army "was a perfect mob," Sheridan ordered Averell to join with Devin's brigade and pressure Early. Averell's command joined Devin's brigade about two miles north of Mount Jackson. There the Union cavalry ran into Ramseur's and Wharton's divisions. In Averell's estimation, the "naturally strong" position, one "strengthened by artificial defenses," did not invite attack.[275] Additionally, Averell received a report from a signal officer that a Confederate brigade or division "was moving around Averell's right." Sheridan encouraged Averell to not "let the enemy bluff you or your command." While Sheridan advised against "rashness," he informed Averell that he did "desire resolution and actual fighting, with necessary casualties before you retire. There must now be no backing or filling by you without a superior force of the enemy actually engaging you."[276]

Despite the urging from his superior, Averell did not feel comfortable making any major attack. That decision cost him his command.[277] Infuriated with Averell's lack of aggressiveness, Sheridan sent a note to the cavalry officer relieving him of division command. About 11:00 p.m. on the twenty-third, Averell read the "impertinent and angry note…relieving me from duty."[278] The news stunned Averell. He explained his disbelief: "An officer who has served the Government nine years, who has suffered from wounds in battle, cannot without any assigned cause or pretext be suddenly relieved from the command of a division whose record tells of nothing but success and victories without having his sensibilities outraged and his reputation jeopardized."[279]

Averell believed that his unwillingness to attack on the twenty-third, which mirrored Torbert's lack of aggressiveness in the Luray Valley, presented Sheridan with the excuse he needed to get rid of Averell. The division commander believed that from the moment Sheridan assumed command in the Shenandoah Valley in early August, he sought a way to remove Averell from his post.[280]

When Sheridan took command in August, he made Torbert his cavalry chief, despite Averell outranking Torbert. While Sheridan knew,

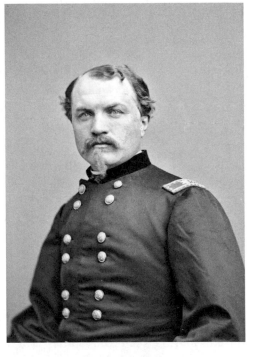

General William W. Averell. *Library of Congress.*

and General Grant warned, that this might create tension, he believed that "if any trouble arose…it could be allayed, or at least repressed…since the different commands would often have to act separately." As Sheridan reflected in his *Personal Memoirs* on Averell's dismissal, he contended that it seemed bound to happen at some point during his tenure in the Shenandoah Valley and that Averell's lack of aggressiveness on the twenty-third convinced Sheridan to do, however unjustifiable some might view it, what he believed right for the army's cohesion. "The removal of Averell was but the culmination of a series of events extending back to the time I assumed command," Sheridan explained. Little Phil continued in defense of his decision: "I therefore thought the interest of the service would be subserved by removing one whose growing indifference might render the best-laid plans inoperative."[281]

By day's end on the twenty-third, Sheridan celebrated his great success in pushing Early off Fisher's Hill but still lamented what might have been realized had his cavalry achieved its objectives. When Sheridan reflected on Fisher's Hill decades after the battle and compared it to his victory at the Third Battle of Winchester, he penned: "The battle of Fisher's Hill was, in a measure a part of the battle of the Opequon…In many ways, however, it was much more satisfactory, and particularly so because the plan arranged on the evening of the 20th was carried out to the very letter by Generals Wright, Crook, and Emory…The only drawback was with the cavalry."[282] Despite the bittersweet taste in Sheridan's mouth, the men in Sheridan's army, especially the three infantry corps, reveled in their second success over Early's army in three days. Reverend John Ripley Adams, the chaplain of the 121st New York, wrote to his wife three days after Fisher's Hill of the army's jubilant spirit: "Thus far the movement has been a glorious and triumphant success…we have dislodged them at Fisher's Hill…It had been…most exciting."[283] A Massachusetts veteran echoed: "A grand victory!…Enemy demoralized."[284]

Some of Sheridan's men believed their success had been so great that Early's command no longer proved a threat in the region. Lieutenant Colonel Benjamin F. Coates, one of Crook's brigade commanders, believed that, as Early's army retreated south toward Port Republic, it would not dare strike against Sheridan's army. Coates explained to his wife the day after Fisher's Hill: "I think now the fighting is certainly over in the Shenandoah valley as the Rebs are driven out."[285] The 29th Maine's Ezekiel Hanson wrote to his mother four days after the battle: "We have no Army in front of us now to oppose our advance."[286] The 121st New York's Sergeant William Remmel also believed, as Early's command withdrew south, that the Confederates no longer presented a challenge to the Union war effort in the Confederacy's breadbasket. "The rebels were never so completely thrashed as they have been this last time...we can get no fight out of them. The rebels will not stand," Remmel explained to his parents several days after the victory.[287]

The timing of Sheridan's success in the valley, coupled with General William T. Sherman's capture of Atlanta on September 2, greatly lifted the nation's spirits and buoyed the morale of Union troops fighting elsewhere.[288] Union artillerist William H. Nichols, attached to the Army of the Potomac stationed at Deep Bottom, Virginia, at the time of Sheridan's victory at Fisher's Hill, could not contain his enthusiasm when he learned of the victory in the Shenandoah Valley. "Another glorious Union victory has been gained," Nichols wrote to his friends. He continued: "Sheridan and his noble army have but again covered themselves with glory...they completed the rout of the foe. Demoralized, broken, stripped of their cannon and so forth, nothing is left them [Early's army] but retreat. The remnants of that boasted army which was to invade the North—was to carry the war to the gates of the Capitol...will return to Richmond, not describing their victories, but heralding this defeat."[289] Some of the officers on General George Gordon Meade's staff thought news of Sheridan's defeat of Early at Fisher's Hill warranted a champagne party. "Sheridan's victory justified a bottle of champagne," recalled Lieutenant Colonel Theodore Lyman.[290]

Some civilian Federal employees, who had been glum about the chances for Union victory in the summer of 1864, now seemed certain that the Confederacy would not be able to do anything to defeat the triumvirate of Grant, Sheridan and Sherman. Horatio Nelson Taft, an employee in the U.S. Patent Office, wrote in his journal: "Considerable progress has been made in the war...Genl. Sheridan who has superseded Hunter in the Shenandoah Valley...has driven them all out of the Valley after two....hard Battles, one at 'Winchester" and one at 'Fisher's Hill'...It looks very much now as though the rebellion is 'caving in'...It is not thought that they can cope with Grant, Sherman, or Sheridan."[291]

When Grant learned of Sheridan's victory at Fisher's Hill he ordered the artillerists of the Army of the Potomac to fire "a salute of hundred guns... the guns being aimed at the enemy around Petersburg." Grant also ordered his other generals "throughout the country" to fire "salutes in honor of his [Sheridan's] victory."[292]

Members of Lincoln's administration, too, beamed with exultation over Sheridan's triumph. Secretary of War Stanton ordered "a salvo of fifteen hundred guns…to celebrate the victory at Fisher's Hill."[293] No one, however, could have been more overjoyed with Sheridan's success than Lincoln. Less than one month before Sheridan delivered his crushing blow to Early, Lincoln believed his chances for reelection seemed so dim that he penned a memorandum to his cabinet members informing them that "it seems exceedingly probable that this Administration will not be re-elected."[294] Sheridan's success now made Lincoln's concern less likely.

Sheridan's victories, combined with those of Sherman, caused Lincoln and his supporters to realize that their greatest weapon in the bid for reelection was not a speech but continued Union success. The *Press*, a Philadelphia newspaper, explained to its readers the political ramifications of Sheridan's victories: "The value of Gen. Sheridan's new victory is not to be measured by prisoners, standards, and guns.…It is a…victory for the supporters of the Union over the real foes and the false friends of the country. It is a new endorsement of Abraham Lincoln, thundered in the Shenandoah Valley…these grand victories inspire the nation with new ardor, and make the platform on which General McClellan stands its laughing stock."[295] About twenty years after the conflict, Grant reflected in his *Personal Memoirs* that Sheridan's "decisive victory" at Fisher's Hill "was the most effective campaign argument made in the canvass."[296]

With Sheridan's victory at Fisher's Hill his celebrity grew in the North. Little Phil's "dashing achievements" in the Shenandoah Valley prompted journalist George Alfred Townsend to believe that news of Sheridan's success "overtopped all" of the "dull infantry endeavors" of the Army of the Potomac.[297] After Fisher's Hill, Sheridan's image decorated the walls of Northern households, and people throughout the Union looked for ways to praise him.[298] Several days after the battle, around thirty thousand Lincoln supporters gathered at New York's Cooper Institute and passed a resolution that lauded Sheridan. It stated, in part, that "resolved, that the thanks of the nation are due to…Sheridan, who…fights Early…up the Valley of the Shenandoah 'striking and doubling up the left flank of the enemy' at Fisher's Hill…and, apparently without a single compunction of conscience, routed the whole rebel army."[299]

As Sheridan's star rose in the aftermath of Fisher's Hill, at least one of Sheridan's subordinates, Colonel Rutherford B. Hayes, wondered if the Northern press might heap too much praise on Sheridan at the peril of neglecting the troops who executed the successful flank attack—the crucial element in Union success. Four days after the battle, Hayes penned his uncle: "Now all the correspondents are with the Sixth and Nineteenth Corps and the cavalry command. General Crook has nobody to write him or his command up. They are of course lost sight of."[300] In the context of 1864, Hayes's observation may have been an overreaction, but it was one that portended a battle for a legacy that would not manifest until after the Civil War's end.

Newspapers throughout the Union in the autumn of 1864, while they noted Sheridan's impeccable generalship, did not lose sight of "the gallant Crook."[301] Other items that celebrated the great victory in the battle's immediate aftermath paid tribute to all elements of the Army of the Shenandoah for their roles in turning the tide in the Union's favor. For example, shortly after the battle, the Washington, D.C. printing firm of G.P. Hardwick produced patriotic writing paper that celebrated Union success in the valley with a poem entitled the "Battle of Winchester." The poem honored not only Sheridan's success at the Third Battle of Winchester but also his victory at Fisher's Hill and paid tribute to all elements of the army, including Crook's corps. In reference to the Eighth Corps, the patriotic poem stated: "Then Crook with his men came up to share the laurels too."[302] Sheridan, likewise, held nothing back in his praise for Crook. Sheridan informed Grant after the battle: "General Crook's command furiously attacked the enemy's line, carrying everything before him."[303]

Hayes's fears, perhaps unwarranted in 1864, became realized when Sheridan wrote his official report of the action in February 1866, after the conflict's end. In the report, Sheridan claimed it was he who conceived the idea for the flank attack, not Crook. While Sheridan's report incensed some, such as Hayes, nothing enraged the veterans of the Eighth Corps more than the publication of Sheridan's *Personal Memoirs* in 1888. Those who fought with Crook at Fisher's Hill believed that Sheridan did not praise Crook and his men enough for their role at that battle. An irate staff officer from Ohio penned in 1896: "I feel that Genl. Sheridan in his memoirs, does not give Crook, Thoburn, and Hayes, the credit which is their due for this glorious victory. In fifteen lines he disposed the whole of Crook's movements and, that, in vain which conveys to the reader's mind that it was of but little consequence." The anger of Crook's veterans increased when it appeared to them that Sheridan paid too much attention to the efforts played by Wright's and Emory's corps at the battle. Captain Russell Hastings, one of Hayes's closest confidants, chastised Sheridan's *Memoirs*: "To the other two corps who were only fighting a *waiting* battle… he gives several pages."[304]

One year after the publication of Sheridan's two-volume recollections, Crook visited the battlefields of Sheridan's 1864 Shenandoah Campaign.

After his visit to Fisher's Hill on December 26, 1889, Crook—once Sheridan's close friend—noted in his diary: "After dinner we…rode over the Fisher's Hill battleground…After examining the grounds and the position of the troops after twenty five years…and in light of subsequent events, it renders Gen. Sheridan's claims…all the more contemptible."[305]

While Sheridan's oversight of Crook's role at Fisher's Hill, coupled with other events, strained the decades-old friendship, Sheridan, at least initially, wanted to make certain that Crook received proper recognition for his role in helping the Army of the Shenandoah achieve success on September 22, 1864. On May 2, 1866, several months after Sheridan submitted his official report of the campaign, Sheridan implored Secretary of War Edwin Stanton to promote Crook to the rank of major general in the regular army for his extraordinary conduct at the Third Battle of Winchester and Fisher's Hill. Sheridan's message, however, seems odd as in late March 1866, Crook received the promotion that Sheridan requested in May.[306]

Although the Battle of Fisher's Hill would eventually stress friendships and raise significant concerns among some Union officers as to how history might judge their role in the engagement, the results of Fisher's Hill presented a different set of issues for General Early's defeated command.

In the days that followed the battle, some of Early's men took pause to reflect on the disaster at Fisher's Hill. They believed the loss at Fisher's Hill had greatly demoralized the entire command. Henry Kyd Douglas observed: "The battle of Fisher's Hill…made the Valley of Virginia, for us, what it had been during Jackson's day for the enemy, a 'Valley of Humiliation.'"[307] Confederate cavalryman John Opie concluded that with the defeat at Fisher's Hill "the *esprit* and *morale* of the army was lost."[308] Buckner Magill Randolph, a veteran of the Forty-ninth Virginia, thought that each of Early's men held confidence in their ability as soldiers but lost faith in the men who stood with them in the ranks. One week after the battle, Randolph wrote to his mother: "Our men are still considerably demoralized…They are not so much dispirited themselves, as that they have lost confidence in each other."[309]

Some of Early's men seemed downtrodden not only because of the loss at Fisher's Hill and defeat three days earlier at the Third Battle of Winchester but also because their losses in the valley came against the backdrop of the collapse of Atlanta. Three days after the battle, General Ramseur penned his wife from Port Republic: "On the 22nd the whole army stampeded without much of a fight…This is a sad blow, coming as it does on the heels of the affair at Atlanta." Ramseur, however, as did other young officers in the

Confederacy, tried to urge his wife and the men under his command to treat the disaster at Fisher's Hill merely as a setback on the road to Confederate victory. "But let us not be discouraged & all will be well," Ramseur implored his wife.[310]

Newspapers in the Confederacy tried to buoy spirits as well. "The fall of Atlanta had already cast a gloom over this community," noted one journalist, "and this reverse [Fisher's Hill] will very much increase it we fear. It should not be so. The fortunes of war are always uncertain, and reverses are, of course, very saddening; but it is unbecoming our people not to shake off their long faces and bring themselves to calmly and resolutely consider the situation…though de-feated today, tomorrow it will retrieve the loss, and laugh at the sad and gloomy people."[311]

Some of the Confederacy's more realistic supporters believed that Early's loss at Fisher's Hill, coupled with General John Bell Hood's dreadful circumstances in Georgia, helped signal the Confederacy's death knell. Winchester's Mary Greenhow Lee confided in her diary on news of Early's defeat at Fisher's Hill: "It has added to the gloom which possesses the town."[312] Famed Confederate diarist Mary Chesnut seemed stunned when she learned about Early's defeat. Chesnut lamented: "Our defeats in the Valley are fearful…These stories of our defeats in the Valley fall like blows upon a dead body."[313]

Amid the gloom of defeat, troops in Early's command and Confederate civilians searched for answers as to how Confederate forces could have been so terribly routed at Fisher's Hill. For some of Early's veterans, such as Captain James Garnett, the defeat happened because God permitted it. "I thought that we would certainly be successful at Fisher's Hill," Garnett observed in his diary two days after the battle, "but Providence has seen fit to order it otherwise."[314] At least one other soldier in Early's army supported this notion. An anonymous Confederate veteran wrote to President Jefferson Davis and contended that Confederate forces in the Shenandoah Valley would not achieve success until the army was placed in the hands of a general who "does not ignore the name of the lord."[315]

While some might have seen the debacle in providential terms, others blamed the Confederate cavalry. General Early stood among the critics of the troopers who defended his western flank. Three days after the battle, Early lashed out against cavalry: "In the affair at Fisher's Hill the cavalry gave way, but it was flanked. This could have been remedied if the troops had remained steady, but a panic seized them…and without being defeated they broke, many of them fleeing shamefully."[316] General Clement Evans, though not a participant in the battle, concurred with Early's assessment. Evans wrote to his wife that the defeat at Fisher's Hill came as a result of "our weak & cowardly cavalry."[317]

Some of Early's command, however, believed the criticism heaped on the Confederate cavalry unfair. Placed in an unenviable position, not given appropriate tools to construct defenses and ill-equipped, a contingent of Early's army thought the circumstances given to General Lomax and his men did not give them an opportunity for success. Henry Kyd Douglas noted after the conflict: "Our cavalry was feeble, badly mounted and badly equipped…whatever ridicule was heaped upon our cavalry…it must be remembered that it was almost impossible, that late in the war, to keep a body of mounted men in even semi-serviceable condition."[318] The Forty-ninth Virginia's Buckner Magill Randolph not only supported Douglas's observation but also contended that the infantry, although seized by a panic at the scene of Lomax's cavalry giving way so quickly, should share the blame. "At Fisher's Hill too," Randolph explained to his mother one week after the battle, "the cavalry are much to blame, tho' the infantry share with them there the general disgrace."[319] One Confederate cavalryman who did "not wish to reproach Gen. Early" believed that had Lomax's command "been properly supported, the result would have been different."[320]

Beyond the Shenandoah Valley and the ranks of Early's army, newspaper editors believed Early's defeat at Fisher's Hill proved a symptom of a much larger problem with the structure of the Confederate military—President Jefferson Davis micromanaged too much. Some believed that if Davis appointed Lee general in chief, Lee would have much more power to address all of the Confederacy's issues, not just those of the Army of Northern Virginia. The *Richmond Enquirer* editorialized that "taking steps to retrieve our fortunes is with Gen. Lee…We need a regular army, with its real and compact organizations, and its firm and unyielding discipline…Congress should recognize this fact, and perfect the organization."[321]

Among all the explanations for the Confederate defeat at Fisher's Hill, no one confronted harsher criticism, aside from Lomax's cavalry, more than General Early. Some of Early's veterans respected his abilities as a fighter and recognized his talents to command a contingent of troops as part of a larger army but did not believe he possessed the necessary skill for independent command in the Shenandoah Valley. Confederate veteran John Opie wrote in disgust decades after the conflict: "General Early, was a brave man, and a good fighter when someone put up the sign boards for him. But, as a commander, he was utterly inefficient and incapable."[322] One of

Early's veterans believed so little in Early that he implored President Davis to remove him from command immediately. The anonymous soldier wrote to Davis—who at the time of Early's defeat was in Georgia attempting to deal with the problems that confronted Hood's army—that he could not know the "exact state of affairs" in the Shenandoah Valley. The disgruntled soldier contended that Early had been drinking during the battle. Although not likely, the veteran, a "soldier since 1861," informed Davis: "This army once the pride of the country has lost its morale… Genl. Early… Has totally unfitted himself by hard drinking to do anything."[323]

The charges of drunkenness reached the ears of the Confederate Congress as well. When South Carolina's Senator James L. Orr learned of the charge, he urged the Confederate Senate to establish a committee to examine Early's conduct in the Shenandoah Valley.[324]

A portion of the valley's civilians also seemed concerned about their fate if Early remained in command. In the aftermath of Fisher's Hill, Early eventually pulled his battered army back to Waynesboro and could do little to stop the next phase of Sheridan's 1864 Shenandoah Campaign—the "Burning." From September 26 to October 8, Sheridan's troops devastated farms and property in Augusta, Rockingham, Shenandoah and Page Counties. Sheridan's directive to lay waste to the Shenandoah adversely impacted not only the valley's inhabitants but also the larger Confederate war effort as two of the four counties targeted by Union torches—Augusta and Rockingham—stood as the top two wheat-producing counties in the Old Dominion.[325] A deeply anxious Sarah L. McComb, a resident of Augusta County, implored President Davis to remove Early from command. She explained: "There will never be any thing but defeat & disaster until Genl Early is relieved of the command…men & Senior officers have lost all confidence in their leader."[326]

Complaints about Early also arrived on the desk of Virginia's governor, William "Extra Billy" Smith. As someone who served under Early's command earlier in the conflict, Smith harbored animosity toward Early but tried his hand at objectivity when urged by some of his constituents to force General Lee to replace the Shenandoah Valley general.[327] The impetus for Smith's communiqué to Lee on October 6 stemmed from a letter Governor Smith received from an unidentifiable source four days earlier. This mysterious Confederate officer, identified by Smith as "an officer who has my entire confidence," informed the governor that Early's debacle at Fisher's Hill caused the army to lose faith in him. "The army once believed him a safe commander," the mysterious officer explained to Smith, "and felt that they could trust to his caution, but unfortunately this has been proven a delusion and they cannot, do not, and will not give him their confidence. He was surprised at Winchester…and Fisher's Hill was the terrible sequence." In this officer's estimation, as had been the case with those who wrote to President Davis, only Early's removal from the Shenandoah Valley offered hope to turn the tide in a region once dominated by Confederate forces. This nameless Confederate officer informed the governor: "I know one thing that I believe the good of the country requires that General Early should not be kept in command of this army; that every officer with whom I have conversed upon the subject is of the same opinion, and I believe it is the sentiment of the army."[328]

Governor Smith informed Lee that he respected Early's qualities as a "brave" and "patriotic" general but believed Early lacked the "qualities for independent command" and suggested that he be replaced with an abler general. Smith recommended General Breckinridge for the post in the Shenandoah Valley.[329]

Lee disagreed with Smith's analysis. The Army of Northern Virginia's commander informed Governor Smith that, from his perspective, Early had "conducted the military operations in the Valley well." Furthermore, Lee informed Smith that he refused any action against Early until Smith lifted the veil from the identity of the Confederate officer who chastised Early. "Justice to General Early requires that I should inform him of the accusations made against him and of the name of his accuser. The matter can then be officially investigated," Lee explained.[330]

Smith did not believe revealing the officer's identity a necessary precondition for Early's termination in the valley. The governor reminded Lee that the accusations against Early came not only from the anonymous Confederate officer but also from residents of the Shenandoah Valley and politicians in the Old Dominion. Smith reminded Lee that, about one week before he sent his note of condemnation to Lee, the two men had had "a conversation with one of the most intelligent citizens of the Valley, residing in the midst of General Early's operations…and…that judgment called for a change in the commander of the Valley army."[331]

Undoubtedly incensed by Smith's bold comments, Lee finally sent the complaint to Secretary of War James A. Seddon. The native Virginian, described as "largely ineffectual" by one historian, perused the documents sent him by Lee.[332] After reviewing the case against Early, Seddon sent the communications to President Davis with the following endorsement: "I have no recommendation to make of any change of commander."[333]

While Smith attempted to make his case against Early, some of Early's men remained steadfast in their support for their beleaguered commander. One week after the battle, a Virginia soldier penned his mother from Waynesboro that, despite defeat and criticism, "I have not lost my confidence in old Jubal."[334]

Lee, too, remained steadfast in his support for General Early. He recognized that Early's numerically inferior army, greatly depleted by casualties at Winchester and Fisher's Hill, would need to be reinforced if it had any chance of maintaining its role of strategic diversion in the Shenandoah Valley. Support came from General Joseph Kershaw's division, as well as General Thomas Rosser's cavalry brigade.[335] However, in retrospect, Lee's support of General Early merely delayed the inevitable. Less than one month after the Confederate disaster at Fisher's Hill, on October 19, 1864, Early's army—despite a promising start—suffered its final catastrophic defeat at the Battle of Cedar Creek and surrendered control of the Breadbasket of the Confederacy to Sheridan's triumphant army.[336]

Chapter Six

"We Are on a Peaceful Visit"

I n the years that followed Sheridan's triumphant campaign in the Shenandoah Valley, veterans of the Army of the Shenandoah reflected on their time in the region and contemplated how their victories, including the smashing success at Fisher's Hill, defined their military legacies. One veteran recalled: "Sheridan's army contained many troops who had unfortunate experiences in the Valley, but the reversal of fortunes in the…autumn of 1864 caused jubilation and erased the memory of painful defeats."[337] In the years that followed the Civil War's end, Sheridan's veterans longed to immortalize their fallen comrades and erect monuments on the valley's battlefields. However, postwar circumstances of animosity spurred in part by Reconstruction and an unwillingness to initially accept the war's consequences made the vision of commemoration in the South nearly impossible for any Union veteran, not just Sheridan's.

After the conflict, many former Confederates in the valley looked negatively on Sheridan and his veterans, as they not only defeated Early's army but also brought significant destruction to the region during the Union army's scorched earth policy that followed Union victory at Fisher's Hill. One year after the conflict's end, Edward Pollard lambasted the Army of the Shenandoah for what it had done in the aftermath of the battle: "The horror and crime in this devastation was remarkable even in Yankee warfare. They impoverished a whole population; they reduced women and children to beggary and starvation; they left the black monuments of Yankee atrocity all the way from the Blue Ridge to the North Mountain."[338]

The attitude among many of the former Confederate supporters in the Shenandoah Valley, however, toward Union veterans began to change by the 1880s. As the region's economy stabilized and crop outputs rose to prewar levels, the region's recovering population began to accept the war's results.[339] What further fueled this emerging sentiment of national reconciliation was that, by the late 1870s and early 1880s, Union veterans began to view the South differently, as former Union veterans and their families made the South a vacation destination. The entire South had evolved, as historian Nina Silber has pointed out, from a battleground into a spot for vacation and relaxation.[340] One observer recalled of this transformation in the Shenandoah: "Instead of a battle field, the Valley of Virginia has been changed to an immense summer resort. Numerous springs and summer hotels dot the mountain sides and there is no more imposing mountain scenery anywhere."[341]

Amid this new climate of reconciliation, the veterans of the Fourteenth New Hampshire—the unit that led the pursuit of Early's command on the night of September 22—discussed the possibility of holding their regimental reunion in Winchester in 1884 to coincide with the twentieth anniversary of the opening of Sheridan's 1864 Shenandoah Campaign. When the Fourteenth New Hampshire's veterans published their proposed itinerary in New England newspapers in the autumn of 1882, it piqued the curiosity of other Union veterans, those who did not serve in the Fourteenth, who viewed this as a tremendous opportunity to organize a reunion of all the Sheridan veterans in the Shenandoah Valley. The widespread interest prompted the Fourteenth New Hampshire's Colonel Carroll Wright and other veterans of the regiment to establish the Sheridan's Veterans' Association (SVA). As interest in

Colonel Carroll Wright, president of the Sheridan's Veterans' Association. *Sheridan's Veterans, 1883.*

the endeavor intensified, Wright, the SVA's president, urged they not wait until 1884 but rather make a visit to their old battlegrounds in 1883 and use Winchester as the headquarters for their "excursion" to the region.[342] Veteran Francis Buffum recalled: "It was the opportunity of a lifetime for the veterans who followed Sheridan to victory, to revisit the scenes of their triumphs, to contrast the dreadful past with the happy present."[343]

After planning, preparation and an incessant stream of communications with Winchester's city council—a group that wholeheartedly embraced the visit—the SVA arrived in Winchester on September 18, 1883. Following the warm reception by the city's residents, including members of Winchester's United Confederate Veterans Camp Number Four, Sheridan's veterans were greeted officially by Winchester's mayor, William Clark. Typical of postwar reconciliation rhetoric, Clark stated that he admired the "gallantry" of the Union veterans in battle. Colonel Wright reciprocated the respectful remarks: "We did not anticipate the grand reception extended us by your government and your citizens…We have come into your beautiful Valley for the second time, now with no scenes of war to make our visit memorable, but with peace in our hearts and with prayers for the welfare of our whole country…we do come as soldiers, to meet brave men who withstood us manfully in battle."[344]

During their weeklong excursion in the Shenandoah Valley, the SVA held ceremonies in Winchester's National Cemetery and the city's Stonewall Confederate Cemetery. Additionally, the veterans visited the battlefields that had defined their legacies. On September 21, the SVA visited the Fisher's Hill battlefield. The veterans strolled over the field and visited the remnants of earthworks constructed by Early's men prior to the battle (traces of Confederate earthworks are still visible on the battlefield today). One Union veteran recalled of the scene: "That was a memorable forenoon's stroll. The group's eager visitors at once thronged the positions held by Early on the afternoon of September 22, 1864. The rifle-pits and the bastions, the earthworks for artillery…are still to be seen in good condition."[345]

The day after their visit to Fisher's Hill, the veterans boarded train cars and began their journey home. As the train steamed north, the veterans reflected on their experience in the valley. Elisha Hunt Rhodes, the SVA's vice-president, believed that the excursion and interaction with former Confederates had done a great deal to move the nation toward healing the wounds of war. Rhodes explained: "I believe in sentiment as a wonderful incentive in human life. Sentiment is sometimes derided, but it is one of the practical impulses of the world. Sentiment develops the strongest and most

beautiful qualities in a man. The excursion grew out of sentiment. By its inspirations we have all been quickened."[346]

Inhabitants of the Shenandoah Valley, too, reflected positively on the SVA's visit. One resident of the valley wrote to the *Boston Globe* in praise of the SVA: "The visit has done more to cement together two sections and to harmonize the differences than all the sermons that have been preached since the war."[347]

Two years after their initial visit, the SVA returned to the Shenandoah Valley. When the veterans arrived in Winchester on September 16, 1885, former Confederates, as they had done in the previous visit, welcomed the veterans warmly. With Confederate veterans as their guides, the SVA again toured their former battlefields, including Fisher's Hill. Even twenty-one years after the battle, the scenic vistas and seemingly impenetrable nature of Early's old position amazed

Ribbon worn by a veteran of the Thirty-fourth Massachusetts during the visit of the Sheridan's Veterans' Association to the Shenandoah Valley in 1883. The Thirty-fourth Massachusetts served in Crook's corps during the battle. Sixteen veterans of the regiment returned to the Shenandoah Valley in 1883 as part of the excursion. *Author's collection.*

Members of the Sheridan's Veterans' Association in 1885 viewing the position defended by General John B. Gordon's division during the battle. *Author's collection.*

the veterans. "This battle-field presents one of the most picturesque views to be found in the Valley," observed a veteran of the Fourteenth New Hampshire, "and one of the toughest spots to assail, as all can testify who stood in the Union ranks when the order to advance was given." Now under a different set of circumstances in 1885, one of the SVA's members recalled that the "party much enjoyed the scramble over the hills and bluffs of this formidable position."[348]

After the SVA's visit to the Shenandoah Valley in 1885, the group never returned to the region again as an organization, although various regimental associations that composed the SVA continued to make the Shenandoah Valley the scene of annual reunions well into the 1900s. While the SVA may have never returned to the region, the spirit of reconciliation that it extended and its visits to Fisher's Hill with former Confederate veterans undoubtedly helped inspire the members of the Stover Camp of Confederate Veterans to organize an annual event at Fisher's Hill. Established on September 15, 1891, the Stover Camp organized its first gathering in the summer of 1892.[349] Local newspapers and written reminiscences by veterans stated that the gathering, which continued well into the 1900s, always attracted large crowds of no fewer than five thousand people.[350]

Each year, the crowd not only contained area residents and former Confederates but also Union veterans. A journalist from the *Baltimore Sun* observed: "Many Union soldiers who fought and bled in the Valley of Virginia…usually journey from the North to attend this great gathering, and they are always recipients of a cordial welcome." Union veterans not only attended but were also active participants in delivering speeches to the crowd about the merits of national unity. Against the backdrop of remarks by Union veterans, those with connections to the former Confederacy urged those in attendance to accept the conflict's results and erase postwar animosity. For example, during the gathering at Fisher's Hill in 1909, Winchester City solicitor, R. Gray Williams, according to a journalist present, "defined the duties of Sons of Confederate Veterans and pledged their determination to hasten the complete reunion of the sections."[351]

Moving forward and aiding in reconciliation's progress, however, did not mean totally ignoring some of the conflict's salient issues. For instance, the year after Williams's comments, Holmes Conrad, a former Confederate officer who served in the Shenandoah Valley in 1864, addressed the crowd, which included Union veterans, and informed them that Virginia, as well as the other ten states that seceded from the Union, were justified in seceding and that Virginia had done "everything possible to avert war." Conrad publicly lambasted President Lincoln during his remarks and contended that Lincoln did nothing to avoid conflict. Despite his incendiary tone, the Union veterans present seemed to shrug off Conrad's comments. One observer noted: "Many Union veterans were in the throngs, as has been customary since the Fisher's Hill event became a reunion of more than passing notice, and nothing, occurred to mar the pleasure of the day."[352]

In addition to speeches by veterans of both sides and the general "fraternizing of the former foes," relic hunting also proved a popular activity for those who ventured to the annual event. A Richmond newspaper correspondent reported, "And every year some souvenir of the fight which took place there is found, consisting of cannon-balls, bullets, and parts of shells."[353]

The members of the Stover Camp not only organized the annual reunions at Fisher's Hill—what one individual referred to as one of "the great occasions of the Valley"—but they also viewed themselves as the guardians of the Fisher's Hill battlefield and served as ambassadors and gracious hosts anytime Union veterans visited the place when not part of the annual gathering each August. For instance, when 110 veterans of the Fifteenth New Jersey visited the battlefield in late May 1907, the Stover Camp ceremonially greeted them at Fisher's Hill. Camp commander R.D. Funkhouser informed the New Jersey veterans: "This is an…honor conferred on me…to welcome you to-day in friendly words and with kindly feelings…after lo, these many

Veterans of the Fifteenth New Jersey and Confederate veterans from Strasburg's Stover Camp gather for a photograph at Fisher's Hill in the spirit of reconciliation in 1907. The Fifteenth New Jersey served in Wright's Sixth Corps. *Author's collection.*

years it affords us great pleasure to meet you under our own vine and fig tree, where none dares to molest you nor make you afraid, and we are not afraid of you either, hence we welcome you most cordially because we are now a united people who jointly possess the grandest country on the globe."[354]

The Fifteenth New Jersey's A.W. Whitehead, the chairman of its visit to the valley, responded to Funkhouser's remarks with similar respect. "It affords me great pleasure to be the one selected from the 'ranks' to reply to this grand and noble address of welcome," Whitehead stated. He continued: "I assure you that we are on a peaceful visit, more so very much than when we last met over forty years ago." In rhetoric typical of postwar reconciliation, Whitehead noted that both Union and Confederate veterans, although each fought for different purposes, had shared difficulties as soldiers in battle and in camp that no one else could ever fathom. Whitehead asserted that those difficulties created an unceasing bond and informed the crowd: "None but those who have been in the front rank, know what war really is." As Whitehead closed his remarks, he thanked not only the Stover Camp veterans for their cordiality but also the ladies of the United Daughters of the Confederacy from the area who attended: "We want to thank you for your very kind…hospitality and the manner in which you have received us who were once your enemies, but we hope now and forever to be your fast friends and comrades. Then to the ladies of your camp—The Daughters

The wives of veterans from the Fifteenth New Jersey gather for a photograph with members of the United Daughters of the Confederacy during the regimental association's visit to Fisher's Hill in 1907. *Author's collection.*

of the Confederacy—do we extend *more* than thanks for your generous repast."[355] Undoubtedly, Whitehead, like other Union veterans in the era of reconciliation, believed it important to pay special recognition to the United Daughters of the Confederacy as many Union veterans believed them not only the guardians of the Confederate past but also the one demographic of the former Confederacy who needed to be won over in order for national unity to truly be achieved. One Union veteran who fought with Sheridan's army and visited the region after the conflict noted of the importance of winning over the Confederate women: "It has always been conceded that the women of the South, who were signally loyal to the cause, have been the most implacable opponents to any steps toward reconciliation, and have been the last to recognize any good as coming from the North."[356] As the New Jersey veterans departed Fisher's Hill, the United Daughters of the Confederacy bade farewell to their Union counterparts with a version of "Dixie." One of the veterans noted that the musical entertainment "was a fitting conclusion to the enjoyable hours spent at Fisher's Hill."[357]

Two years after the veterans of the Fifteenth New Jersey visited Fisher's Hill, the importance of the battlefield, due not only to its significance to Civil War history in the region but also to its symbolic importance as a gathering place for veterans of both sides to advance the cause of national reconciliation, compelled a group of businessmen in Shenandoah County, Virginia, to take

Bronze tablet commemorating the Battle of Fisher's Hill, incorrectly stating the number of troops engaged at the battle. *Photograph by author.*

steps to purchase and preserve the site and then maintain the battlefield as a tourist attraction and permanent gathering point for veterans of both armies. In early September 1909, the *Baltimore Sun* reported: "Steps have been taken by a number of wealthy men of Shenandoah County, Virginia, to buy the Fisher's Hill battlefield grounds…and convert them into a military park. It is proposed to make this park the home of a number of Confederate reunions…This is a very interesting project, and a movement for the preservation of one of the most historic battlefields of the Old Dominion." For reasons unclear, the plan never materialized. Despite the inability of those businessmen to establish Fisher's Hill as a military park, the veterans of both armies continued to gather on the site for years after the deal fell through.[358]

Although unable to be preserved in the early 1900s as some Shenandoah County residents hoped, the Virginia Statewide Battlefields Markers' Association recognized the battlefield's importance, along with twenty-five others in Virginia, when it placed a bronze tablet on a fieldstone base to memorialize the battle and the role Confederate soldiers played in the losing effort. The marker incorrectly places Sheridan's overall strength at sixty thousand and states that the singular cause of the disasters was due to "the advantage of overwhelming numbers."

While that marker, which still stands today near the Valley Pike, marked the battlefield for future generations, it failed to recognize what is arguably the site's greatest contribution to history—a stage for postwar reunion and reconciliation. Although the battlefield, considerable portions of which today have been preserved through the efforts of the Civil War Trust and Shenandoah Valley Battlefields Foundation, marks a significant Union victory and stands as a testament to heroism and sacrifice of soldiers on both sides, its significant role as a place for former foes to gather and bind up the wounds of war cannot be overstated. Perhaps it was former Confederate general and later governor of Virginia Fitzhugh Lee—who incidentally held a campaign rally during his successful gubernatorial run in 1885 at Fisher's Hill—who best captured what the years of reunion and reconciliation activities among Union and Confederate veterans at places like Fisher's Hill meant for the country: "Such reunions result in producing a fraternal feeling among the sections and strengthening the union of States...the South is marching steadily forward and...she is not chanting miseries...but is waving the star-spangled banner and hopes the 'blood shirt' will be furled forever."[359]

An interview conducted nearly thirty years after the conflict's end by Emma Howard Wright with an unidentifiable resident of Fisher's Hill lends credence to Lee's observation and illustrates that, while a place like Fisher's Hill might have helped cement Union victory in the Civil War, the postwar activities of former enemies on the battlefield and acts of reconciliation by Union veterans helped strengthen the bonds of the nation. The anonymous "old farmer" informed Wright: "For some time after the close of the war there were very bitter feelings in my heart against the North, but these have all died away now. I have grown to look upon it in this light—that they fought, as we did, for what they considered right."[360]

Notes

PREFACE

1. Samway, *Walker-Percy*, 71.
2. Walker, *Vermont Brigade*, 10.

INTRODUCTION

3. Ibid.

CHAPTER ONE

4. Carpenter, *History of the Eighth*, 164.
5. For further discussion of the use of the valley as a diversionary theater of war in the spring of 1862 and summer of 1864, respectively, see Noyalas, *Stonewall*; Patchan, *Shenandoah Summer*.
6. For further discussion on Grant's mentality in the summer of 1864 see Noyalas, "Early's Costliest Victory," 65–73.
7. Grant, *Personal Memoirs*, 316–17.
8. Snell, *From First to Last*, 92, 151, 199.
9. Wert, *Sword of Lincoln*, 387; Gallagher, *Struggle*, 41–43.
10. For an examination of the Third Battle of Winchester see Beck and Delauter, *Third Battle of Winchester*.
11. Ezekiel H. Hanson to mother, September 21, 1864, papers of Ezekiel H. Hanson, Nicholas P. Picerno private collection, Bridgewater, VA.
12. Woodbury, *Second Rhode Island*, 298.
13. Julia Chase diary, September 21, 1864, Julia Chase Collection, Stewart Bell Jr. Archives, Handley Regional Library, Winchester, VA. All items from this repository hereafter cited as HL.

14. Styple, *Writing and Fighting*, 293; For further discussion of the tenuous nature of life for African Americans in the lower Shenandoah Valley see Noyalas, *Two Peoples*; Berkey, "War in the Borderland," 172–223.

15. Jordan, *Civil War Journals*, 403.

16. Fitts, "Fight at Fisher's Hill," 430.

17. Sheridan, *Personal Memoirs*, 33.

18. Opie, *Rebel Cavalryman*, 251.

19. Casler, *Four Years*, 234.

20. Gordon, *Reminiscences*, 324.

21. Colt, *Defend the Valley*, 338; Noyalas, "Portrait of a Soldier," 87; medical discharge, Robert Barton Family Papers, HL.

22. U.S. War Department, *War of the Rebellion*, series 1, volume 43, part 1, 555, hereafter cited as OR1.

23. Early, *Memoir*, 98.

24. Pollard, *Lost Cause*, 596.

25. The best statistical analysis of Early's army after the Third Battle of Winchester can be found in Gallagher, *Shenandoah Valley*, 166.

26. Early, *Narrative*, 429.

27. Buck, "Battle," 338.

28. Wert, *From Winchester*, 29.

29. Early, *Memoir*, 98.

30. *New York Herald*, September 27, 1864.

31. For a discussion of the generalship of Robert E. Rodes and what his loss meant to Early see Krick, *Smoothbore*, 139–43.

32. Gallagher, *Shenandoah Valley*, 165; Davis, *Breckinridge*, 454–55.

33. Early, *Narrative*, 429–30.

34. Douglas, *I Rode*, 312.

35. General Bryan Grimes to his wife, September 26, 1864, quoted in Cowper, *Extracts*, 68–69.

36. OR1, 47.

37. Haines, *History of the Fifteenth*, 264.

38. Ibid., 475; Patchan, "Battle of Fisher's Hill," 20.

39. Fravel, "Between the Lines," 176.

40. Ibid.

41. *New York Herald*, February 13, 1865.

42. Rodenbough, *From Everglade*, 357.

43. Fitts, "Fight at Fisher's Hill," 431.

44. Sheridan, *Personal Memoirs*, 34.

45. Kennon, "Valley Campaign," 45.

46. DuPont, *Campaign of 1864*, 135.

47. Kennon, "Valley Campaign," 45; Williams, *Hayes*, 267.

48. Williams, *Hayes*, 267. There seems to be some disagreement among previous studies of Fisher's Hill as to where the evening council of war actually occurred. While all are in agreement that it took place in a headquarters tent near the Valley Pike, historian Scott Patchan places the meeting in the front yard of George Hupp's residence in Strasburg. Shenandoah County historian Richard Kleese places the meeting in a tent on the grounds of the Stickley Farm just south of the intersection of the Valley Pike and Cedar Creek. Jeffry Wert, in his study of the 1864 Shenandoah Campaign, intimates that it might have also occurred in the vicinity of the Stickley Farm. There appears to be no conclusive evidence to firmly contend where the council of war occurred. For more on these debates, see Patchan, "Battle," 20; Kleese, *Shenandoah County*, 75; Wert, *From Winchester*, 111.

49. Magid, *George Crook*, 258–59.

50. Lang, *Loyal West Virginia*, 334.

51. Russell Hastings, "Fisher's Hill,"Russell Hastings Papers, Rutheford B. Hayes Presidential Center, Fremont, OH, 4. Items from this repository hereafter cited as RBH.

52. Crook handwritten manuscript autobiography, Crook-Kennon Papers, United States Army Military History Institute, Carlisle, PA; Cooling, *Jubal Early's Raid*, 202. At the fight at Cool Spring, Wright ordered Colonel Joseph Thoburn's division to attack Early's Confederates. Thoburn's men went into the fight alone, and when they needed support, Wright refused to send any additional troops. For an examination of this battle and Wright's ill-advised decision see Patchan, *Shenandoah Summer*, 60–104.

53. Hastings, "Fisher's Hill," Russell Hastings Papers, RBH, 3–5

54. Johnson, *From a "Whirlpool,"* 98.

55. Crook commanded twenty infantry regiments. Ten of those regiments were from western Virginia (West Virginia after 1863).

56. Hastings, "Fisher's Hill," Russell Hastings Papers, RBH, 4–5; Williams, *Hayes*, 268.

57. Lang, *Loyal West Virginia*, 334.

58. Johnson, *From a "Whirlpool,"* 99.

59. Wert, *From Winchester*, 112; Simson, *Custer*, 27.

60. OR1, 142.

61. Walker, *Vermont Brigade*, 111.

62. Fitts, "Fight at Fisher's Hill," 431.

63. *Albany Evening Journal*, September 28, 1864.

64. Fitts, "Fight at Fisher's Hill," 431.

Chapter Two

65. OR1, 428, 499.

66. Haines, *History of the Fifteenth*, 265.

67. Wert, *From Winchester*, 113.

68. U.S. War Department, *War of the Rebellion*, series 1, volume 43, part 2, 117–18, hereafter cited as OR2. Stanton's message to Sheridan stated, "Please accept for yourself and your gallant army the tanks of the President and this Department for your great battle and brilliant victory of yesterday. The President has appointed you a brigadier general in the Regular Army, and you have been assigned to the permanent command of the Middle Division. One hundred guns were fired here at noon to-day in honor of your victory."

69. McDonald, *Make Me a Map*, 230.

70. Jones, *Civil War Memoirs*, 143.

71. Taylor, *With Sheridan*, 397.

72. OR1, 274. According to Captain McCartney, his battery fired twenty-five rounds of solid shot and thirty-two rounds of case shot; Sheridan, *Personal Memoirs*, 36.

73. Sheridan, *Personal Memoirs*, 36.

74. Ibid.; Walker, *Vermont Vermont Brigade*, 114.

75. OR1, 199.

76. Joseph Warren Keifer, *Slavery and Four Years of War: A Political History of Slavery in the United States, Together with a Narrative of the Campaigns and Battles of the Civil War in Which the Author Took Part: 1861–1865* (New York: G.P. Putnam's Sons, 1900) 2: 119.

77. OR1, 264. This definition of a bullpen protection as employed on Flint Hill can be found in Geier, Lotts and Whitehorne, *Flint Hill* 52.

78. Keifer, *Slavery*, 119.

79. OR1, 152, 199.

80. Mark, *Red*, 294.

81. Taylor, *With Sheridan*, 397.

82. OR1, 152.

83. Pond, *Shenandoah Valley*, 175; Mark, *Red*, 294; Wert, *From Winchester*, 117.

84. Walker, *Vermont Brigade*, 115.

85. OR1, 282.

86. Ibid.

87. Patchan, "Battle," 21.

88. OR1, 282.

89. Beecher, *Record*, 433.

90. Ibid.; Fitts, "Fight at Fisher's Hill," 433.

91. Taylor, *With Sheridan*, 397, 400. The location of Keister's house is based off Taylor's and this source's descriptions.

92. Ibid., 400.

93. Sheridan, *Personal Memoirs*, 36.

94. Johnson, *From a "Whirlpool,"* 99.

95. *Springfield Republican*, November 29, 1886.

96. Rosenblatt and Rosenblatt, *Hard Marching*, 259.

97. Early, *Narrative*, 430.

CHAPTER THREE

98. OR1, 282.

99. Hanaburgh, *History*, 153.

100. OR1, 297.

101. Ibid.; Wert, *From Winchester*, 117.

102. OR1, 282.

103. Jordan, *Civil War Journals*, 404.

104. Gould, *History*, 508–09.

105. Ibid., 509.

106. Fitts, "Fight at Fisher's Hill," 433–34.

107. Taylor, *With Sheridan*, 401.

108. Wright, "Signal," 399; Hutchinson and Kilby, *Fisher's Hill*, 3–10.

109. OR1, 282.

110. Krick, *Civil War Weather*, 135–38. This conclusion is based off weather records reported by Krick.

111. OR1.

112. Ibid. The mill is also identified, at times, as Spangler's Mill.

113. Sheridan, *Personal Memoirs*, 36.

114. Schmitt, *General*, 130.

115. Walker, *Vermont Brigade*, 116–17.

116. Ibid., 116.
117. OR1, 283.
118. Gould, *History*, 509; Jordan, *Civil War Journals*, 404–05.
119. OR1, 283.
120. Ibid.; Patchan, "Battle of Fisher's Hill," 23.
121. OR1, 283.
122. Hanaburgh, *History*, 153.
123. Jordan, *Civil War Journals*, 405.
124. Gould, *History*, 510; OR1, 283.
125. Taylor, *With Sheridan*, 402; OR1, 274.
126. Croushore, *Volunteer's*, 194.
127. Ibid. While DeForest does not positively identify with whom specifically he had this discussion, he intimates that it more than likely was a member of Sheridan's staff.
128. Ibid., 195.
129. Wert, *From Winchester*, 118; OR1, 223.
130. Keifer, *Slavery*, 120.
131. Ibid.
132. *Richmond Dispatch*, June 14, 1891.
133. OR1, 254.
134. Keifer, *Slavery*, 120.
135. *Richmond Dispatch*, June 14, 1891.
136. Walker, *Vermont Brigade*, 117.
137. OR1, 556; Early, *Narrative*, 430.
138. OR1, 363.
139. Walker, *Vermont Brigade*, 117.
140. OR1, 499.
141. Wildes, *Record*, 181.
142. *Springfield Republican*, November 29, 1886.
143. Runge, *Four Years*, 99.
144. Cowper, *Extracts*, 69; Allen, *Lee's*, 194. Grimes was not the only member of the Confederate command who had little faith in the ability of the Confederate cavalry in the Shenandoah Valley. For further discussion on this point, see Gallagher, *Struggle*, 77–106.
145. *Richmond Dispatch*, June 14, 1891.
146. Cowper, *Extracts*, 69.
147. Ibid., Allen, *Lee's*, 194.
148. *Richmond Dispatch*, June 14, 1891.
149. Ibid.

150. Garnett, "Diary," 8; Gallagher, *Stephen*, 148.

151. OR1, 556; Gallagher, *Shenandoah Valley*, 169.

152. Patchan, "Battle of Fisher's Hill," 24; OR1, 363.

153. Johnson, *From a "Whirlpool,"* 99.

154. Wildes, *Record*, 181.

155. *Springfield Republican*, November 29, 1886.

156. OR1, 363.

157. Johnson, *From a "Whirlpool,"* 101.

158. Wildes, *Record*, 181.

159. Hastings, "Fisher's Hill," Russell Hastings Papers, RBH, 10.

160. O'Ferrall, *Forty Years*, 118.

161. OR1, 611.

162. Baker, Civil War Memoirs, Virginia Military Institute Manuscript Archives, Lexington, VA.

163. Patchan, "Battle of Fisher's Hill," 25.

164. OR1, 611.

165. Cox, *Address*, 43.

166. Wert, *From Winchester*, 123.

167. O'Ferrall, *Forty Years*, 119; Gallagher, *Shenandoah Valley*, 174.

168. Buck, "Battle," 338.

169. Thacker, *French*, 172.

170. Beck, *Third Alabama*, 128. Early's congratulatory communiqué to Battle stated in part that "to you belongs the honor of saving the day in the enemy's first attack at Winchester."

171. *Richmond Dispatch*, June 14, 1891.

172. Watts, "Gen. Battle and a Stolen Yankee Colt: Being a Confederate Veteran's Answer to the Query of How the South Would Have Acted Toward the North in Victory" *Richmond Times-Dispatch*, May 3, 1936; Beck, *Third Alabama*, 122.

173. OR1, 370.

174. Schmitt, *General*, 131.

175. Runge, *Four Years*, 100.

176. Ibid.

177. Wise, *Long Arm*, 888–89.

178. OR1, 378; Earley, *I Belonged*, 153.

179. Johnson, *From a "Whirlpool"*, 102.

180. Schmitt, *General*, 131; Patchan, *Shenandoah Summer*, 80–81. Patchan contains further discussion of Ricketts's failed support of Crook at the Battle of Cool Spring.

181. Cowper, *Extracts*, 69.

182. Ibid., 71.

183. Early, *Narrative*, 430.

184. McDonald, *Make Me a Map*, 231.

185. Buck, *With the Old Confeds*, 115.

186. Ibid.

CHAPTER FOUR

187. Keifer, *Slavery*, 122.

188. Swinfen, *Ruggles' Regiment*, 57.

189. OR1, 213, 153; Buell, *Cannoneer*, 279.

190. *Vermont Journal*, October 15, 1864.

191. Walker, *Vermont Brigade*, 119.

192. Buell, *Cannoneer*, 279. Isaac O. Best writes in his regimental history of the 121st New York that the men climbed "up the steep bank on the other side through the brush and briars. We used them to pull ourselves up by." Best, *History of the 121st New York State Infantry*, 186.

193. OR1, 217. Major Stephen Fletcher of the Seventh Maine Infantry wrote of this incident in his report of the battle: "After…commencing to ascend the hill, shots from the First Brigade [Warner's] compelled us to halt…As soon as it was made known to them we again moved forward, charging upon the rebel works."

194. Ibid., 203, 192.

195. Haines, *History of the Fifteenth*, 267.

196. Fonerden, *Brief History*, 54.

197. OR1, 218.

198. Walker, *Vermont Brigade*, 120.

199. OR1, 218.

200. Ibid., 221.

201. Schmitt, *General*, 132.

202. OR1, 249, 258; Evans, *Confederate Military*, 706.

203. Jones, *Civil War Memoirs*, 144; Jones, *Lee's Tiger's*, 217.

204. Jones, *Civil War Memoirs*, 144.

205. *Richmond Dispatch*, June 14, 1891.

206. Jones, *Lee's Tigers*, 217–18. Speech of Jubal Early to veterans of the Louisiana Brigade.

207. Haines, *History of the Fifteenth*, 267.

208. Carpenter, *History of the Eighth*, 200.
209. Buffum, *Memorial*, 249.
210. Carpenter, *History of the Eighth*, 200.
211. Ewer, *Third Massachusetts*, 210.
212. Gould, *History*, 511–12.
213. Colonel Edward Molineux to sister Nan, n.d., Colonel Edward Molineux Papers, Fred Molineux Private Collection, Pittstown, NJ.
214. *New York Times*, April 10, 1904.
215. Buffum, *Memorial*, 250.
216. McDonald, *Make Me a Map y*, 231.
217. Early, *Narrative*, 430; Wildes, *Record*, 183.
218. Haines, *History of the Fifteenth*, 267.
219. Clark, *One Hundred*, 230.
220. Wildes, *Record*, 183–84.
221. Clark, *One Hundred*, 230. Evidence does indicate that some of Early's men became prisoners of war at Fisher's Hill because they simply gave up and refused to fight for what they believed was a losing effort. For an example of this, see Wert, *From Winchester*, 126–27.
222. Bushong, *Old Jube*, 241–42.
223. Hanaburgh, *History*, 155.
224. Clark, *One Hundred*, 230.
225. Haines, *History of the Fifteenth*, 267.
226. Buffum, *Memorial*, 251.
227. Hastings, "Fisher's Hill," Russell Hastings Papers, RBH, 13.
228. Colonel Edward Molineux to sister Nan, September 28, 1864, Colonel Edward Molineux Papers, Fred Molineux Private Collection, Pittstown, NJ.
229. OR1, 332.
230. Buffum, *Memorial*, 252.
231. McDonald, *Make Me a Map*, 231.
232. Buck, *With the Old Confeds*, 115; Bean, *Stonewall's Man*, 210.
233. OR1, 332.
234. *Richmond Dispatch*, June 14, 1891.
235. Buffum, *Memorial*, 252.
236. Gould, *History*, 514.
237. OR1, 332.
238. Buffum, *Memorial*, 253.
239. Buck, *With the Old Confeds*, 115; Douglas, *I Rode*, 312.
240. Ibid., 312–13. Pendleton married Kate Corbin on December 29, 1863. Freeman, *Lee's Lieutenants*, 584.

241. McDonald, *Make Me a Map*, 231.

242. Douglas, *I Rode*, 275, 313.

243. Lee, *Memoirs*, 372.

244. Johnson, *University Memorial*, 656.

245. Ibid.

246. Lee, *Memoirs*, 372.

247. Bean, *Stonewall's Man*, 210.

248. Ibid.; Lee, *Memoirs*, 372.

249. Bean, *Stonewall's Man*, 211, 216–17.

250. Strader, *Civil War Journal*, 420.

251. Early, *Memoir*, 100.

252. Johnson, *University Memorial*, 657.

253. Gould, *History*, 514–15.

254. Ibid., 515.

255. Sheridan, *Personal Memoirs*, 42.

256. Buffum, *Memorial*, 255.

257. Haines, *History of the Fifteenth*, 268.

258. OR1, 59. The great difficulty in determining the total casualty figures for the Army of the Shenandoah at Fisher's Hill is that while the Sixth and Nineteenth Corps reported specific casualties for this battle, General Crook's Eighth Corps combined their casualties from the Third Battle of Winchester and Fisher's Hill into an aggregate. For further discussion on the slight difference in casualty figures see Wert, *From Winchester*, 129; Patchan, "Battle of Fisher's Hill," 50.

259. OR1, 556.

260. Sharpe, *Shenandoah County*, 49.

261. Wright, "Old Farm-House," 223. Wright gave no indication as to the identity of the farmer. However, it is believed from oral history sources that this family farm might have been owned by the Barr family. For further discussion see Patchan "Battle of Fisher's Hill," 59.

262. Obituary clipping for Mrs. Rebecca M. (Funkhouser) Glaize, Funkhouser Collection, David J. Garms, Fairfax, VA.

263. Ibid., 27.

264. Sheridan, *Personal Memoirs*, 40.

CHAPTER FIVE

265. OR1, 48.

266. Buck, *Sad Earth*, 284–85; Simson, *Custer and the Front Royal Executions*, 28.

267. Simson, *Custer*, 47; OR1, 428.

268. Munford, "Reminiscences," 454.

269. Ibid.

270. OR1, 428; Coffey, *Sheridan's Lieutenants*, 64; Longacre, *Lee's Cavalrymen*, 314–15.

271. Wert, *From Winchester*, 132.

272. Sheridan, *Personal Memoirs*, 42.

273. OR1, 499, 500.

274. Sheridan, *Personal Memoirs*, 43.

275. OR1, 500.

276. Sheridan, *Personal Memoirs*, 44.

277. McDonald, *Make Me a Map*, 231–32. Hotchkiss wrote in his journal on September 23: "The enemy's cavalry came up and threw a few shells, but no advance was made."

278. William Woods Averell, diary, September 23, 1864, William Woods Averell Papers, New York State Library, Manuscripts and Special Collections, Albany, NY.

279. OR1, 500.

280. Ibid.

281. Sheridan, *Personal Memoirs*, 44–45. For further discussion about Sheridan's decision to remove Averell from command and that Sheridan had, in fact, not been justified in doing so, see Wittenberg, *Little Phil*, 109–15.

282. Sheridan, *Personal Memoirs*, 41–42.

283. Adams, *Memorial*, 157.

284. Howe, *Passages*, 74.

285. Lieutenant Colonel Benjamin F. Coates to wife, September 23, 1864, Coates Papers, RBH.

286. Ezekiel H. Hanson to mother, September 26, 1864, Nicholas P. Picerno Private Collection, Bridgewater, VA.

287. Bender, *Like Grass*, 123-124.

288. Woodworth, *Grant's Lieutenants*, 164–65; Thomas and Hyman, *Stanton*, 329; Leech, *Reveille*, 348.

289. Taber, *"Orleans Battery"*, 198.

290. Lowe, *Meade's Army*, 269.

291. Diary of Horatio Nelson Taft, October 3, 1864, Library of Congress, Washinton, D.C.
292. Grant, *Personal Memoirs*, 331–32.
293. Lang, *Loyal West Virginia*, 335.
294. Basler, *Collected Works*, 514.
295. *The Press*, September 24, 1864, September 27, 1864.
296. Grant, *Personal Memoirs*, 332. For further discussion of the issues of the Presidential Election of 1864 and the role Sheridan's success played in it see Flood, *1864*, 300–01.
297. Townsend, *Rustics in Rebellion*, 244–45.
298. Wert, *From Winchester*, 141.
299. *Daily Evening Bulletin*, September 28, 1864.
300. Williams, *Diary*, 513.
301. *Daily Evening Bulletin*, September 28, 1864.
302. "The Battle of Winchester, September 19th 1864," Jonathan A. Noyalas private collection, Martinsburg, WV.
303. OR1, 26.
304. Hastings, "Fisher's Hill," Hastings Papers, RBH, 13–14.
305. Schmitt, *General*, 134.
306. Ibid., 136; Magid, *George Crook*, 262. For further discussion of the feud between Sheridan and Crook see Wittenberg, *Little Phil*, 106–09.
307. Douglas, *I Rode*, 313.
308. Opie, *Rebel Cavalryman*, 252.
309. Buckner Magill Randolph to mother, September 29, 1864, Randolph Family Papers, 1786–1970, Virginia Historical Society, Richmond, VA.
310. Kundahl, *Bravest of the Brave*, 279. For further discussion of this phenomenon see Gallagher, *Confederate War*, 106.
311. Unidentified Southern journalist quoted in *New York Herald*, September 25, 1864.
312. Strader, *Civil War Journal*, 419.
313. Woodward, *Mary Chesnut's*, 647–48.
314. Garnett, "Diary," 8. For further examination of Confederates using Providence as a means of explaining and coping with defeat, see Rable, *God's Almost*, 389–90.
315. Crist, *Papers*, 110.
316. OR1, 558.
317. Stephens, *Intrepid Warrior*, 450. For further criticism of Early's cavalry, see Gallagher, *Struggle*, 77–106.
318. Douglas, *I Rode*, 314.

319. Buckner Magill Randolph to mother, September 29, 1864, Randolph Family Papers, 1786–1970, Virginia Historical Society, Richmond, VA.

320. "Confederate Cavalry" *Confederate Veteran*, 52.

321. For examples of Davis's meddling even after Lee became general in chief, see Davis, *Jefferson Davis*, 596; *Richmond Enquirer*, September 26, 1864.

322. Opie, *Rebel Cavalryman*, 252.

323. Crist, *Papers*, 110.

324. Bushong, *Old Jube*, 245.

325. Noyalas, *"Give the Enemy"*, 30–31. For a full treatment of this destructive period, see Heatwole, *Burning*.

326. Sarah L. McComb to Jefferson Davis, October 24, 1864, quoted in Crist, *Papers*, 117.

327. Bushong, *Old Jube*, 244.

328. OR1, 894.

329. Ibid.

330. Ibid., 895.

331. Ibid., 896.

332. Davis, *Look Away*, 348.

333. OR1, 893.

334. Buckner Magill Randolph to mother, September 29, 1864, Randolph Family Papers, 1786–1970, Virginia Historical Society, Richmond, VA.

335. Dowdey, *Wartime Papers*, 856–57.

336. For further discussion of the Battle of Cedar Creek see Noyalas, *Battle*.

Chapter Six

337. Kennon, "Valley Campaign," 159.

338. Pollard, *Southern*, 109.

339. Geier and Potter, *Archaeological*, 241–42.

340. Silber, *Romance*, 66–70.

341. King and Derby, *Camp-Fire*, 513. For further examination of the valley's emerging role as a tourist destination at this time, see Hofstra and Reitz, *Great Valley*, 180–82. For additional discussion on the emergence of reconciliation sentiment at this time, see Blight, *Race*, 198–206.

342. The veterans were mindful that rhetoric played an important part in postwar reconciliation. Referring to it as an excursion portrayed it more as a vacation-like experience rather than a military reunion,

which had the air of a conquering army returning to the scene of its former battlefield triumphs.

343. Buffum, *Sheridan's Veterans*, 7.

344. Ibid, 25, 27.

345. Ibid., 86.

346. Ibid., 113.

347. *Boston Daily Globe*, September 27, 1883.

348. Buffum, *Sheridan's Veterans*, 86.

349. Kleese, *Shenandoah County*, 116; *Baltimore Sun*, August 8, 1909.

350. "Stover Camp," *Confederate Veteran*, 27.

351. *Baltimore Sun*, August 8, 1909.

352. Ibid., August 7, 1910.

353. *Times*, June 11, 1902.

354. *Pilgrimage*, 33.

355. Ibid., 35–36.

356. *Boston Daily Globe*, September 27, 1885. For further discussion on the influence of Confederate women in the postwar period, see Janney, *Burying*, 93–106.

357. *Pilgrimage*, 36.

358. *Baltimore Sun*, September 2, 1909.

359. Ibid., September 19, 1885.

360. Wright, "Old Farm-House," 223, 225.

Bibliography

Manuscript Collections

David J. Garms, Fairfax, VA.
Funkhouser Collection.

Fred Molineux, Pittstown, NJ.
Colonel Edward Molineux Papers.

Jonathan A. Noyalas, Martinsburg, WV.
"The Battle of Winchester, September 19th, 1864."

Library of Congress, Washington, D.C.
Diary of Horatio Nelson Taft.

Linden A. Fravel/Stone House Foundation, Stephens City, VA.
"Between the Lines: The Civil War Diaries, Letters and Memoirs of the Steele Family of Newton/Stephen City, VA, 1861 to 1864." Unpublished manuscript current as of January 19, 2003.

New York State Library, Manuscripts and Special Collections, Albany, NY.
William Woods Averell Papers.

Nicholas P. Picerno, Bridgewater, VA.
Papers of Ezekiel H. Hanson.

Rutherford B. Hayes Presidential Center, Fremont, OH.
   Coates Papers.
   Hastings Papers.

Stewart Bell Jr. Archives, Handley Regional Library, Winchester, VA.
   Julia Chase Collection.
   Robert Barton Family Papers.

United States Army Military History Institute, Carlisle, PA.
   Crook-Kennon Papers.

Virginia Historical Society, Richmond, VA.
   Randolph Family Papers, 1786–1970.

Virginia Military Institute Manuscript Archives, Lexington, VA
   Isaac Norval Baker Civil War Memoirs. 18th Virginia Cavalry, Company F.

GOVERNMENT DOCUMENTS

U.S. War Department. *War of the Rebellion: A Compilation of the Official Records of the Union and Confederate Armies.* 128 vols. Washington, D.C.: U.S. Government Printing Office, 1880–1901.

PUBLISHED PRIMARY SOURCES

Adams, John R. *Memorial and Letters of Reverend John R. Adams, D.D.* N.p.: privately printed, 1890.

Basler, Roy P., ed. *The Collected Works of Abraham Lincoln.* Vol. 7. New Brunswick, NJ: Rutgers University Press, 1953.

Beck, Brandon H., ed. *Third Alabama!: The Civil War Memoir of Brigadier General Cullen Andrews Battle, CSA.* Tuscaloosa: University of Alabama Press, 2000.

Beecher, Harris H. *Record of the 114th Regiment, N.Y.S.V.: Where It Went, What It Saw, and What It Did.* Norwich, NY: J.F. Hubbard Jr., 1866.

Bender, Robert Patrick, ed. *Like Grass Before the Scythe: The Life and Death of Sergeant William Remmel, 121ˢᵗ New York Infantry*. Tuscaloosa: University of Alabama Press, 2007.

Best, Isaac O. *History of the 121ˢᵗ New York State Infantry.* Chicago, IL: Jas. H. Smith, 1921.

Buck, Lucy Rebecca. *Sad Earth, Sweet Heaven: The Diary of Lucy Rebecca Buck*. Birmingham, AL: Buck Publishing Co., 1992.

Buck, Samuel D. "Battle of Fisher's Hill." *Confederate Veteran* 2, no. 11 (November 1894): 338.

———. *With the Old Confeds: Actual Experiences of a Captain in the Line*. Baltimore, MD: H.E. Houck & Co., 1925.

Buell, Augustus. *The Cannoneer: Recollections of Service in the Army of the Potomac*. Washington, D.C.: National Tribune, 1890.

Buffum, Francis H. *A Memorial of the Great Rebellion: Being a History of the Fourteenth Regiment New Hampshire Volunteers*. Boston, MA: Franklin Press, 1882.

———. *Sheridan's Veterans: A Souvenir of Their Two Campaigns in the Shenandoah Valley, the One, of War, in 1864, the Other of Peace, in 1883, Being the Record of the Excursion to the Battle-Fields of the Valley of Virginia, September 15–24, 1883*. Boston, MA: W.F. Brown & Co., 1883.

———. *Sheridan's Veterans Number II: A Souvenir of Their Third Campaign in the Shenandoah Valley, 1864, 1883, 1885*. Boston, MA: W.F. Brown and Co., Printers, 1886.

Carpenter, George N. *History of the Eighth Vermont Volunteers, 1861–1865*. Boston, MA: Press of Deland and Barta, 1886.

Casler, John O. *Four Years in the Stonewall Brigade*. Girard, KS: Appeal Publishing, 1906.

Clark, Orton S. *The One Hundred and Sixteenth Regiment of New York State Volunteers*. Buffalo, NY: Printing House of Matthews & Warren, 1868.

Colt, Margaretta Barton. *Defend the Valley: A Shenandoah Family in the Civil War*. Oxford: Oxford University Press, 1994.

"The Confederate Cavalry at Fisher's Hill." *Confederate Veteran* 3, no. 2 (1895): 51–52.

Cowper, Pulaski, comp. *Extracts of Letters of Major-General Bryan Grimes, to His Wife*. Raleigh, NC: Alfred Williams & Co., 1884.

Cox, William R. *Address on the Life and Character of Major General Stephen D. Ramseur*. Raleigh, NC: E.M. Uzell, 1891.

Crist, Lynda Lasswell, ed. *The Papers of Jefferson Davis*. Vol. 11. Baton Rouge: Louisiana State University Press, 2003.

Croushoure, James E., ed. *A Volunteer's Adventures: A Union Captain's Record of the Civil War; John William DeForrest*. Baton Rouge: Louisiana State University Press, 1996.

Douglas, Henry Kyd. *I Rode with Stonewall*. Chapel Hill: University of North Carolina Press, 1940.

Dowdey, Clifford, ed. *The Wartime Papers of R.E. Lee*. New York: Bramhall House, 1961.

DuPont, Henry A. *The Campaign of 1864 in the Valley of Virginia and the Expedition to Lynchburg*. New York: National Americana Society, 1925.

Early, Jubal A. *A Memoir of the Last Year of the War for Independence in the Confederate States of America*. Columbia: University of South Carolina Press, 2001.

———. *Narrative of the War Between the States*. Philadelphia, PA: Lippincott, 1912.

Evans, Clement A. *Confederate Military History: A Library of Confederate States History in Seventeen Volumes*. Vol. 4. Wilmington, NC: Broadfoot, 1987.

Ewer, James K. *The Third Massachusetts Cavalry in the War for the Union*. Maplewood, MA: Historical Committee of the Regimental Association, 1903.

Fitts, James F. "The Fight at Fisher's Hill." *Galaxy* 5, no. 4 (1868): 427–38.

Fonerden, C.A. *A Brief History of the Military Career of Carpenter's Battery*. New Market, VA: Henkel, 1911.

Garnett, James M. "Diary of Captain James M. Garnett." *Southern Historical Society Papers* 27 (1899): 1–16.

Gordon, John B. *Reminiscences of the Civil War*. Baton Rouge: Louisiana State University Press, 1993.

Gould, John M. *History of the First, Tenth, Twenty-Ninth Maine Regiment*. Portland, ME: Stephen Berry, 1871.

Grant, Ulysses S. *Personal Memoirs of U.S. Grant*. New York, NY: Charles L. Webster, 1886.

Haines, Alanson A. *History of the Fifteenth Regiment New Jersey Volunteers*. New York, NY: Jenkins and Thomas, 1883.

Hanaburgh, D.H. *History of the One Hundred Twenty-Eighth Regiment, New York Volunteers*. Poughkeepsie, NY: Press of Enterprise Publishing Co., 1894.

Haynes, E.M. *A History of the Tenth Regiment, Vermont Volunteers: With Biographical Sketches of the Officer Who Fell in Battle and a Complete Roster*. N.p.: Tenth Vermont Regimental Association, 1870.

Howe, Henry Warren. *Passages from the Life of Henry Warren Howe, Consisting of Diary and Letters Written During the Civil War, 1861–1865: A Condensed History of the Thirtieth Massachusetts Regiment and Its Flags, Together with Genealogies of the Different Branches of the Family*. Lowell, MA: Courier-Citizen Co., Printers, 1899.

Johnson, Mary E., ed. *From a "Whirlpool of Death…to Victory": Civil War Remembrances of Jesse Tyler Sturm, 14th West Virginia Infantry*. Charleston: West Virginia Division of Culture and History, 2002.

Jones, S.C. *Reminiscences of the Twenty-Second Iowa Volunteer Infantry: Giving Its Organization, Marches, Skirmishes, Battles, and Sieges.* Iowa City, IA, 1907.

Jones, Terry L., ed. *The Civil War Memoirs of Captain William J. Seymour: Reminiscences of a Louisiana Tiger.* Baton Rouge: Louisiana State University Press, 1991.

Jordan, William B., ed. *The Civil War Journals of John Mead Gould.* Baltimore, MD: Butternut and Blue, 1997.

Keifer, Joseph Warren. *Slavery and Four Years of War: A Political History of Slavery in the United States, Together with a Narrative of the Campaigns and Battles of the Civil War in Which the Author Took Part: 1861–1865.* New York: G.P. Putnam's Sons, 1900.

Kennon, Lieutenant L.W.V. "The Valley Campaign of 1864: A Military Study." *Papers of the Military Historical Society of Massachusetts: The Shenandoah Campaigns of 1862 and 1864 and the Appomattox Campaign 1865.* Vol. 6. Boston: Military Historical Society of Massachusetts, 1907.

King, W.C., and W.P. Derby, comps. *Camp-Fire Sketches and Battle-Field Echoes.* Springfield, MA: King, Richardson and Co., 1886.

Kundahl, George G., ed. *The Bravest of the Brave: The Correspondence of Stephen Dodson Ramseur.* Chapel Hill: University of North Carolina Press, 2010.

Lang, Theodore F. *Loyal West Virginia: From 1861 to 186; with an Introductory Chapter on the Status of Virginia for Thirty Years Prior to the War.* Baltimore, MD: Deutsch Publishing Co., 1895.

Lee, Susan P. *Memoirs of William Nelson Pendleton, D.D.: Rector of Latimer Parish, Lexington, Virginia; Brigadier-General, C.S.A.; Chief of Artillery, Army of Northern Virginia.* Philadelphia, PA: J.B. Lippincott, 1893.

Lowe, David W., ed. *Meade's Army: The Private Notebooks of Lieutenant Colonel Theodore Lyman.* Kent, OH: Kent State University Press, 2007.

Mahon, Michael G., ed. *Winchester Divided: The Civil War Diaries of Julia Chase & Laura Lee.* Mechanicsburg, PA: Stackpole Books, 2002.

Mark, Penrose G. *Red, White, and Blue Badge: Pennsylvania Veteran Volunteers; A History of the 93rd Regiment, Known as the "Lebanon Infantry" and "One of the 300 Fighting Regiments" from September 12th 1861 to June 27th 1865.* Harrisburg, PA: Auginbaugh Press, 1911.

McDonald, Archie P., ed. *Make Me a Map of the Valley: The Civil War Journal of Stonewall Jackson's Topographer.* Dallas, TX: Southern Methodist University Press, 1973.

Munford, Thomas T. "Reminiscences of Cavalry Operations." *Southern Historical Society Papers* 12 (1884): 343–50, 447–59.

O'Ferrall, Charles T. *Forty Years of Active Service.* New York, NY: Neale Publishing Co., 1904.

Opie, John N. *A Rebel Cavalryman with Lee Stuart and Jackson.* Chicago: W.B. Conkey, 1899.

Pilgrimage of the Fifteenth Regiment New Jersey Volunteers' Veteran Association to Gettysburg and the Shenandoah Valley, May 21ˢᵗ to 25ᵗʰ, 1907. Elizabeth, NJ: Henry Cook Printshop, 1907.

Pollard, Edward A. *The Lost Cause: A New Southern History of the War of the Rebellion.* New York: E.B. Treat and Co., 1866.

———. *Southern History of the War: The Last Year of the War.* New York: Charles B. Richardson, 1866.

Rodenbough, Theophilus F. *From Everglade to Canon with the Second Dragoons (Second United States Cavalry).* Norman: University of Oklahoma Press, 2000.

Rosenblatt, Emil, and Ruth Rosenblatt, eds. *Hard Marching Every Day: The Civil War Letters of Wilbur Fisk, 1861–1865.* Lawrence: University Press of Kansas, 1992.

Runge, William H., ed. *Four Years in the Confederate Artillery: The Diary of Private Henry Robinson Berkeley.* Richmond: Virginia Historical Society, 1991.

Schmitt, Martin F., ed. *General George Crook: His Autobiography.* Norman: University of Oklahoma Press, 1986.

Sheridan, Philip H. *Personal Memoirs of P.H. Sheridan.* New York: Charles L. Webster & Co., 1888.

"Stover Camp Confederate Monument" *Confederate Veteran* (July 1898): 27.

Strader, Eloise C., ed. *The Civil War Journal of Mary Greenhow Lee (Mrs. Hugh Holmes Lee) of Winchester, Virginia.* Winchester, VA: Winchester-Frederick County Historical Society, 2011.

Styple, William B., ed. *Writing and Fighting the Civil War: Soldier Correspondence to the New York Sunday Mercury.* Kearny, NJ: Belle Grove Publishing, 2000.

Swinfen, David B. *Ruggles' Regiment: The 122ⁿᵈ New York Volunteers in the American Civil War.* Hanover, NH: University Press of New England, 1982.

Taber, Thomas R., ed. *The "Orleans Battery": A History of the 17ᵗʰ New York Light Artillery in the War of the Rebellion.* Albion, NY: Almeron Press, 2012.

Taylor, James. *With Sheridan up the Shenandoah Valley in 1864: Leaves from a Special Artists Sketch Book and Diary.* Dayton, OH: Morningside House, 1989.

Thacker, Victor L. *French Harding Civil War Memoirs.* Parsons, WV: McClain Printing Co., 2000.

Townsend, George Alfred. *Rustics in Rebellion: A Yankee Reporter on the Road to Richmond, 1861–1865.* Chapel Hill: University of North Carolina Press, 1950.

Walker, Aldace F. *The Vermont Brigade in the Shenandoah Valley: 1864.* Burlington, VT: Free Press Association, 1869.

Wildes, Thomas F. *Record of the One Hundred and Sixteenth Regiment Ohio Infantry Volunteers in the War of the Rebellion.* Sandusky, OH: I.F. Mack & Bro., Printers, 1884.

Williams, Charles Richard, ed. *Diary and Letters of Rutherford Birchard Hayes*. Vol. 2. Columbus: Ohio State Archaeological and Historical Society, 1922.

Woodbury, Augustus. *The Second Rhode Island Regiment: A Narrative of Military Operations*. Providence, RI: Valpey, Angell & Co., 1875.

Woodward, C. Vann, ed. *Mary Chestnut's Civil War*. New York: Essential Classics of the Civil War, 1981.

Wright, Emma Howard. "The Old Farm-House at North Mountain." *Blue and Gray: The Patriotic American Magazine* (March 1893): 223–25.

———. "The Signal from Round Hill." *Blue and Gray: The Patriotic American Magazine* (July–December, 1893): 389–401.

NEWSPAPERS

Albany Evening Journal
Baltimore Sun
Boston Daily Globe
Daily Evening Bulletin
National Tribune
New York Herald
New York Times
Pennsylvania Daily Telegraph
The Press [Philadelphia]
Richmond Dispatch
Richmond Enquirer
Richmond Times-Dispatch
Soldiers' Journal
Springfield Republican
Times
Vermont Journal

SECONDARY SOURCES

Allen, T. Harrell. *Lee's Last Major General: Bryan Grimes of North Carolina*. Mason City, IA: Savas, 1999.

Bean, W.G. *Stonewall's Man: Sandie Pendleton*. Chapel Hill: University of North Carolina Press, 1959.

Beck, Brandon H., and Roger U. Delauter Jr. *The Third Battle of Winchester.* Lynchburg, VA: H.E. Howard, 1997.

Blight, David W. *Race and Reunion: The Civil War in American Memory.* Cambridge, MA: Belknap Press, 2001.

Bushong, Millard K. *Old Jube: A Biography of General Jubal A. Early.* Boyce, VA: Carr Publishing Co., 1955.

Coffey, David. *Sheridan's Lieutenants: Phil Sheridan, His Generals, and the Final Years of the Civil War.* Lanham, MD: Rowman and Littlefield, 2005.

Coffin, Charles Carleton. *Freedom Triumphant: The Fourth Period of the War of the Rebellion.* New York: Harper & Brothers, 1890.

Cooling, Benjamin F. *Jubal Early's Raid on Washington, 1864.* Baltimore, MD: Nautical and Aviation Publishing, Co., 1989.

Davis, William C. *Breckinridge: Statesman, Soldier, Symbol.* Baton Rouge: Louisiana State University Press, 1974.

————. *Jefferson Davis: The Man and His Hour: A Biography.* New York: Harper Collins, 1991.

————. *Look Away! A History of the Confederate States of America.* New York: Free Press, 2002.

Earley, Gerald L. *I Belonged to the 116th: A Narrative of the 116th Ohio Volunteer Infantry during the Civil War.* Westminster, MD: Heritage Books, 2007.

Flood, Charles Bracelen. *1864: Lincoln at the Gates of History.* New York: Simon & Schuster, 2009.

Freeman, Douglas Southall. *Lee's Lieutenants: A Study in Command.* Vol. 3. New York: Charles Scribner's Sons, 1944.

Gallagher, Gary W. *The Confederate War: How Popular Will, Nationalism, and Military Strategy Could Not StaveOff Defeat.* Cambridge, MA: Harvard University Press, 1997.

————. *Stephen Dodson Ramseur: Lee's Gallant General.* Chapel Hill: University of North Carolina Press, 1985.

Gallagher, Gary W., ed. *The Shenandoah Valley Campaign of 1864.* Chapel Hill: University of North Carolina Press, 2006.

————. *Struggle for the Shenandoah: Essays on the 1864 Valley Campaign.* Kent, OH: Kent State University Press, 1991.

Geier, Clarence R., and Stephen R. Potter, eds. *Archaeological Perspectives on the American Civil War.* Gainesville: University Press of Florida, 2000.

Geier, Clarence, Stephen Lotts and Joseph W.A. Whitehorne. *The Flint Hill Parcel at Fisher's Hill: A Cultural Resource Assessment; Report Submitted to the Shenandoah Valley Battlefields Foundation.* Harrisonburg, VA: Department of Sociology and Anthropology, 2007.

Heatwole, John L. *The Burning: Sheridan in the Shenandoah Valley*. Charlottesville, VA: Rockbridge Publishing, 1998.

Hofstra, Warren R., and Karl Reitz, eds. *The Great Valley Road: Shenandoah Landscapes from Prehistory to the Present*. Charlottesville: University of Virginia Press, 2010.

Hutchinson, John D., V, and Phoebe Kilby. *Fisher's Hill & Tom's Brook Battlefields Preservation Plan*. Woodstock, VA: Sympoetica, 2005.

Janney, Caroline E. *Burying the Dead But Not the Past: Ladies' Memorial Associations & The Lost Cause*. Chapel Hill: University of North Carolina Press, 2008.

Johnson, John Lipscomb, comp. *The University Memorial: Biographical Sketches of Alumni of the University of Virginia who Fell in the Confederate War*. Baltimore, MD: Turnbull Bros., 1871.

Jones, Terry L. *Lee's Tigers: The Louisiana Infantry in the Army of Northern Virginia*. Baton Rouge: Louisiana State University Press, 1987.

Kleese, Richard B. *Shenandoah County in the Civil War: The Turbulent Years*. Lynchburg, VA: H.E. Howard, 1992.

Krick, Robert K. *Civil War Weather in Virginia*. Tuscaloosa: University of Alabama Press, 2007.

—————. *The Smoothbore Volley that Doomed the Confederacy: The Death of Stonewall Jackson and Other Chapters on the Army of Northern Virginia*. Baton Rouge: Louisiana State University Press, 2002.

Leech, Margaret. *Reveille in Washington: 1860–1865*. New York: Harper & Brothers, 1941.

Longacre, Edward G. *Lee's Cavalrymen: A History of the Mounted Forces of the Army of Northern Virginia*. Mechanicsburg, PA: Stackpole Books, 2002.

Magid, Paul. *George Crook: From the Redwoods to Appomattox*. Norman: University of Oklahoma Press, 2011.

McPherson, James M. *This Mighty Scourge: Perspectives on the Civil War*. Oxford, UK: Oxford University Press, 2007.

Noyalas, Jonathan A. *The Battle of Cedar Creek: Victory from the Jaws of Defeat*. Charleston, SC: The History Press, 2009.

—————. "Early's Costliest Victory: The Second Battle of Kernstown and Its Impact on Union Strategy in the Shenandoah Valley, 1864" *Winchester-Frederick County Historical Society Journal* 15 (2003): 65–79.

—————. "Portrait of a Soldier: The Confederate Military Service of Private Robert T. Barton, 1861–1862." *Winchester-Frederick County Historical Society Jounral* 16 (2004): 73–94.

—————. *Stonewall Jackson's 1862 Valley Campaign: War Comes to the Homefront*. Charleston, SC: The History Press, 2010.

————. *Two Peoples, One Community: The African American Experience in Newtown (Stephens City), Virginia, 1850–1870*. Stephens City, VA: Stone House Foundation, 2007.

Noyalas, Jonathan A., ed. *"Give the Enemy No Rest!": Sheridan's 1864 Shenandoah Campaign*. New Market, VA: Shenandoah Valley Battlefields Foundation, 2007.

Patchan, Scott C. "The Battle of Fisher's Hill." *Blue & Gray* 24 no. 5 (2008): 6–8, 19–27.

————. *Shenandoah Summer: The 1864 Valley Campaign*. Lincoln: University of Nebraska Press, 2007.

Pond, George E. *The Shenandoah Valley in 1864*. Edison, NJ: Castle Books, 2002.

Rable, George C. *God's Almost Chosen Peoples: A Religious History of the American Civil War*. Chapel Hill: University of North Carolina Press, 2010.

Samway, Patrick, ed. *Walker-Percy: Sign Posts in a Strange Land*. New York: Farrar, Straus and Giroux, 1991.

Sharpe, Hal F. *Shenandoah County in the Civil War: Four Dark Years*. Charleston, SC: The History Press, 2012.

Silber, Nina. *The Romance of Reunion: Northerners and the South, 1865–1890*. Chapel Hill: University of North Carolina Press, 1993.

Simson, Jay W. *Custer and the Front Royal Executions of 1864*. Jefferson, NC: McFarland, 2009.

Snell, Mark A. *From First to Last: The Life of Major General William B. Franklin*. New York: Fordham University Press, 2002.

Stephens, Robert Grier, Jr. *Intrepid Warrior: Clement Anselm Evans: Confederate General from Georgia, Life, Letters, and Diaries of the War Years*. Dayton, OH: Morningside, 1992.

Thomas, Benjamin P., and Harold M. Hyman. *Stanton: The Life and Times of Lincoln's Secretary of War*. New York: Alfred A. Knopf, 1962.

Wert, Jeffry D. *From Winchester to Cedar Creek: The Shenandoah Campaign of 1864*. Mechanicsburg, PA: Stackpole Books, 1997.

————. *The Sword of Lincoln: The Army of the Potomac*. New York: Simon & Schuster, 2005.

Williams, Charles Richard. *The Life of Rutherford Birchard Hayes: Nineteenth President of the United States*. Vol. 1. Boston, MA: Houghton Mifflin, 1914.

Williams, T. Harry. *Hayes of the Twenty-Third: The Volunteer Civil War Officer*. Lincoln: University of Nebraska Press, 1965.

Wise, Jennings Cropper. *The Long Arm of Lee: The History of the Artillery of the Army of Northern Virginia*. New York: Oxford University Press, 1959.

Wittenberg, Eric J. *Little Phil: A Reassessment of the Civil War Leadership of General Philip H. Sheridan*. Washington, D.C.: Brassey's, 2002.

Woodworth, Steven E., ed. *Grant's Lieutenants: From Chattanooga to Appomattox*. Lawrence: University Press of Kansas, 2008.

DISSERTATIONS

Berkey, Jonathan M. "War in the Borderland: The Civilians' Civil War in Virginia's Lower Shenandoah Valley." PhD diss., Pennsylvania State University, 2003.

Index

U

Unionists, Shenandoah Valley 18

W

Walker, Aldace 9, 13, 45

Warner, Colonel James 34, 35, 64, 65,
        68, 69

Waynesboro, Virginia 97, 99

Wells, Colonel George 59, 60

Wharton, General Gabriel 26, 61, 68,
        74, 75, 89

Wheaton, General Frank 35, 39, 40,
        63, 65, 67

Wickham, General Williams C. 22, 85

Wildes, Colonel Thomas F. 50, 54, 55

Wiley, Lieutenant Robert W. 69

Wilson, General James 23, 29, 85

Winchester, Virginia and the Third
        Battle 10, 13, 18, 20, 23, 24, 27,
        30, 57, 81, 84, 90, 91, 93, 94,
        95, 98, 99, 102, 103, 104, 106

Winston, Colonel John 61

Woodstock, Virginia 79, 81, 82, 88

Wright, Emma Howard 82

Wright, General Horatio G. 26, 27, 28,
        29, 30, 31, 32, 33, 34, 35, 38,
        39, 42, 43, 44, 47, 49, 63, 64,
        65, 76, 83, 90, 93, 102, 103, 110

About the Author

Jonathan A. Noyalas is assistant professor of history and director of the Center for Civil War History at Lord Fairfax Community College in Middletown, Virginia. He is the author or editor of nine books on Civil War–era history and has contributed scores of articles, essays and reviews to a variety of publications, including *Civil War Times, America's Civil War, Hallowed Ground, Blue and Gray* and *Civil War News*. Professor Noyalas has served as historian for a variety of historical projects, such as

Photograph by Brandy Noyalas.

Civil War historian for the National Park Service's historic resource study at Cedar Creek and Belle Grove National Historical Park, content expert for the Civil War Trust's Cedar Creek Battle App and consultant for *National Geographic*'s three-part documentary series "Civil Warriors," which debuted in the United States in April 2012. Active in battlefield preservation in the Shenandoah Valley, he serves as chair of the Shenandoah Valley Battlefields Foundation's committee on interpretation and education.

Visit us at
www.historypress.net

....

This title is also available as an e-book